Croner's G DIRECT RESPONSIBILITIES

Robert Spicer

CRONER PUBLICATIONS LIMITED

Croner House, London Road,
Kingston upon Thames
Surrey KT2 6SR

Telephone: 081-547 3333

First published 1993

Published by
Croner Publications Ltd,
Croner House,
London Road,
Kingston upon Thames,
Surrey KT2 6SR
Tel: 081-547 3333

British Library Cataloguing in Publication Data
A CIP Catalogue Record for this book
is available from the British Library

ISBN: 1 85524 186 2

Typeset by ROM-Data Corporation Ltd, Falmouth, Cornwall
Printed by Whitstable Litho Ltd, Whitstable, Kent

Contents

Introduction

The aim of this book is to provide an outline guide to the legal obligations and liabilities of company directors. It does not intend to provide an exhaustive account of the law, but rather to highlight the most significant areas which are likely to cause problems and to point out possible trends in the development of the law. Many of the rules dealing with directors' responsibilities are highly technical and complex. Some of them cannot reasonably be simplified, and are set out in full below. Advice on the detailed application of such rules should be sought from a suitably qualified lawyer or accountant.

Summaries of the most recent relevant cases in each area of law are provided, with the aim of illustrating recent trends and giving guidance on the current approach of the courts. For example, it emerges from an analysis of the recently decided cases that the most active area of litigation is that of disqualification of directors, and aspects of insolvency law, where there has been a massive expansion of case law in recent years.

Company law has been described as the cornerstone of capitalism. The modern limited company has played a crucial role in the economic and social development of the United Kingdom. The advantages of limited liability for entrepreneurial activity are balanced, to some extent, by strict rules governing the behaviour of directors. Current economic conditions, with high levels of insolvencies and the phenomenon of the "phoenix" company, are reflected in the range of cases coming before the courts.

The trend towards increasing personal responsibility of directors is increasing, not only in general company law terms, but also in relation to environmental protection, health and safety at work, financial services and general criminal law.

Most recently, the Cadbury Report on the financial aspects of corporate governance has made a number of proposals for far reaching changes in the way in which directors control their companies' financial affairs.

The role of the company director will vary according to the type of company, and it is difficult to generalise about this role. From a legal point of view directors are, as a general rule, agents of the company with all the implications of the law of agency arising from that role. They may also be employees subject to the general law of employment. Further, in some respects they may be compared with trustees.

There is no simple statement of directors' duties, but a basic principle is that directors must apply skill and care, and must act in good faith in the interests of the company. Many of the duties and responsibilities set out below are related to this principal duty.

Nor is there a legal definition of a director. The closest to a definition in law comes from a judge, Sir George Jessel, who said in the nineteenth century that directors were:

> *"... merely commercial men managing a trading concern for the benefit of themselves and all other shareholders in it".*

Note: Throughout this volume, unless otherwise stated, words imparting the masculine gender include the feminine.

Summary: Directors' General Legal Duties

- To exercise reasonable skill and care.
- Not to let their own interest conflict with that of the company.
- To give proper time and attention to the company.
- Not to make a secret profit.
- Not to misapply the company's property.
- To act bona fide for the benefit of the company as a whole.

1 What is a Company?

Statutes

The legislation dealing with companies, mainly the Companies Act 1948, was consolidated in the Companies Act 1985. This is a very lengthy statute, dealing with most aspects of company law. It lays down minimum standards for the conduct of directors. The Insolvency Act 1986 and the Company Directors Disqualification Act 1986 have tightened up and expanded the rules in relation to directors' responsibilities, particularly where their companies go out of business.

These statutes make even non-executive directors liable for considerable financial penalties and the possibility of disqualification for up to 15 years.

A number of other Acts of Parliament have considerable significance for the responsibilities of directors. These include the Health and Safety at Work etc Act 1974, which provides a code for ensuring the welfare of employees, and the Employment Protection (Consolidation) Act 1978 which contains detailed rules in relation to the rights of employees. These may affect directors in their role as employer as well as employee, and are considered in Chapter 6.

In relation to dishonest actions by directors, the key statute is the Theft Act 1968.

Summary: Companies Acts Rules Affecting Directors

- Declarations of interest in contracts with the company.
- Approval of property transactions with the company.
- Restrictions on loans made to directors by the company.
- Disclosure of directors' shareholdings in the company.

Scope of Company Law

A massive body of statute and case law has grown up since the sixteenth century in respect of registered companies. The rules governing duties and responsibilities of company directors has evolved as an integral part of this mass of law. Many of the decided cases dealing with directors can only be fully understood in their historical context, since English law has never been fully codified, despite the introduction of massive statutes.

Limited Companies

Most companies have limited liability, that is, the liability of the members is limited to the nominal value of the shares held by them. The liabilities of the business belong to the company rather then its members. The main advantages of this, apart from purely financial considerations, are set out below.

The Advantages of Limited Liability

- Taxation–this is outside the scope of this book. Reference should be made to detailed practitioner textbooks. See *Further Reading.*
- Business respectability–companies may be more easily accepted by the business community because of the strict rules governing their financial affairs, and the availability of information about the way in which they are run.
- Public companies can offer their shares for sale to the public (subject to strict conditions) and this is a most useful way of raising capital for expansion.
- The legal personality of a company is not affected by the death or resignation of its members. It thus has stability and continuity which are considerable commercial advantages.

If the company becomes insolvent then a shareholder's personal assets are not available to meet the company's outstanding debts. But there are two major exceptions to this, the basic rule of English company law.

- Persons or institutions lending money to a new company will often insist on guarantees backed by a charge on personal property.
- If the company becomes insolvent, then proceedings may be brought against directors with the aim of establishing personal responsibility for the debts of the company. In general, these proceedings will succeed if the liquidator accepts that the conduct of the directors contributed to the insolvency.

Corporate Personality

A company is an artificial legal person. It is separate from its directors and shareholders. This is the basis of English company law, and confers a number of privileges in the business context. But one price for these privileges is a detailed body of rules dealing with the duties and responsibilities of company directors.

The key case in this area is *Salomon v Salomon* (1897). S formed a company in which he held the vast majority of the shares. He sold his business to the company in return for the shares and debentures held by him, thus making himself a secured creditor. The company went into liquidation. The unsecured creditors tried to recover their money from S himself on the basis that there was no difference between him and the company. They failed. The company was a separate legal entity. The creditors' claims were against the company and not against S in person. The advantages of this principle are that direct proceedings may not, as a rule, be brought against individual members of the company. There are also tax advantages.

This "veil of incorporation" may be lifted in circumstances prescribed by statute, and the courts are also prepared to make individual company members liable for the debts of the company on public policy and other grounds.

Memorandum of Association

This is a document which sets out the purposes for which the company is formed. It states the objects of the company.

It is important for directors to ensure that the company does not act outside the scope of these objects, because if it does then there may be a breach of the *ultra vires* rule, with significant consequences for them. (See Chapter 4.)

Memorandum of Association

The memorandum must state the following:

- the name of the company
- the situation of the registered office in England or Wales
- the objects of the company
- a statement of limited liability
- the amount of the company's share capital.

Articles of Association

This is a document containing a body of rules dealing with the company's internal affairs. A specimen set of Articles, known as "Table A", is provided by statutory instrument. Table A deals with a whole range of matters affecting directors. If a company does not have its own Articles, then Table A will apply. During the formation of a company, it is most important for the powers and duties of directors as stated in Table A to be examined, and any necessary special provisions inserted. In particular, the following matters should be considered:

- Share capital?
- Meetings?
- Alternate directors?
- Powers of directors?
- Delegation of powers?
- Appointment?
- Removal?
- Remuneration?

- Maximum number of directors?
- Borrowing powers?
- Retirement?
- Dismissal?

Name of Company

The choice of a company name is limited by a number of points set out below.

Choosing a Company Name

- It must not duplicate or be too similar to the name of another company. Duplication may give rise to liability for the tort of "passing off".
- The name must not be offensive or imply a connection with the Government.
- In the case of a public company the words "public limited company" or "plc" must appear at the end of the name. Where the company is private, the word "Limited" or "Ltd" must appear at the end.

The name may be changed by special resolution. Any such change must be registered.

Europe

Membership of the EEC, and the advent of the single market, has raised potentially very wide implications for company law. It is outside the scope of this book to discuss these matters in detail, but company administrators must be aware of the ever-increasing flow of European materials. The following matters are of particular significance:

- The EEC Harmonization Programme has made slow progress towards co-ordinating company law throughout the EEC.

- A number of Directives are in force, dealing with the *ultra vires* rule (See Chapter 4); share capital and dividends; and accounts.
- The development of European Economic Interest Groupings, which enable flexible arrangements for joint activities among European companies.

2 Becoming a Director

Appointment

The general rule is that the method of appointing directors (and, indeed, removing them) is set out in the Articles. The first directors of a new company must be named in the statement on application for registration of the company. Subsequent appointments are usually made by existing directors, under the terms of the Articles. Some Articles stipulate that a person must have a share qualification before they can be appointed.

A recent case on appointment is *Lee Panavision v Lee Lighting* (1991). In that case it was stated that where shareholders aim to appoint new directors, the existing directors have no power to pass a resolution removing all managing powers from the new directors.

Anyone may be a director, with the following exceptions:

- Special rules in the Articles of Association. Table A provides the following:
  - prohibition by statute
  - bankruptcy
  - mental disorder
  - resignation by notice
  - absence from board meetings for more than six months.
- Disqualification. (See Chapter 5.)
- Aged over 70.

Register

Directors of new companies must register personal details on Form 10 (see page 12). Persons appointed directors of existing companies must complete Form 288 (see page 16).

Checklist: Powers of Directors (Subject to Articles of Association)

- Make decisions as to calls on shares not fully paid up.
- Refuse registration of transfers of shares.
- Claim indemnity for costs of legal actions on behalf of company.
- Make decisions as to availability of accounts to members of company.
- Call extraordinary general meetings.
- Delegate powers.
- Enter into loan arrangements.
- Create mortgages or charges over company property.
- Appoint a managing director.
- Declare dividends.
- Excercise power of forfeiture of shares.

Where a company is listed on the Stock Exchange appointments must be notified to the Stock Exchange. Personal details must also be recorded on the company's own Register of Directors and Secretaries.

Details on Business Letters

There is no legal requirement for the names of directors to appear on business stationery. But if the name of one director is given, all the others *must* appear.

Legal Nature of Office

As a corporate personality, the activities of a company are controlled primarily by the general meeting of shareholders. But powers of day-to-day management are delegated from this meeting to the board of directors. Public companies must have at least two directors, and private companies at

least one. A director is an "officer of the company". This is the key concept in relation to legal responsibilities.
A company officer is the person in law regarded as accountable for the actions of the company. The directors, as officers of the company, are responsible for the company carrying out its numerous statutory duties. If the company fails to fulfil its legal obligations, then the directors are, as a general rule, personally liable.

Directors are not, by virtue of their office, employees of the company. This is important in three ways.

- They are not entitled as of right to privileges granted to employees.
- There may be problems with regard to preferential debts in a receivership or winding-up.
- They may not be covered by the statutory provisions dealing with employment law (See Chapter 6).

Locus Standi to make Applications

The matter of whether, and in what circumstances, a director may make applications to a court was considered in *A.L.I. Finance Ltd v Havelet Leasing Ltd* (1992). The plaintiff had obtained injunctions against a number of companies and against their managing director in person. The managing director sought to apply on behalf of one of the companies to have the terms of the injunctions varied. The High Court ruled that there was no reason in principle why, in an appropriate case, a director of a company involved in litigation should not be allowed to become a party to it, so that he could, on his own behalf, make an application in relation to orders made against that company.

Also, in the exercise of the inherent power of the court to regulate its own proceedings so as to maintain its character as a court of justice, and as a matter of discretion, the exceptional circumstances merited the grant of Liberty to the director to address the court on behalf of the companies as well as on his own behalf.

Figure 1: Companies Form 10

COMPANIES HOUSE

10

Statement of first directors and secretary and intended situation of registered office

This form should be completed in black.

CN — For official use

Company name *(in full)*

Registered office of the company on incorporation.

RO

Post town

County/Region

Postcode

If the memorandum is delivered by an agent for the subscribers of the memorandum mark 'X' in the box opposite and give the agent's name and address.

Name

RA

Post town

County/Region

Postcode

Number of continuation sheets attached

To whom should Companies House direct any enquiries about the information shown in this form?

Postcode

Telephone

Extension

Page 1

Company Secretary *(See notes 1 - 5)*

Name

*Style/Title	CS
Forenames	
Surname	
*Honours etc	
Previous forenames	
Previous surname	

Address AD

Usual residential address must be given. In the case of a corporation, give the registered or principal office address.

Post town

County/Region

Postcode Country

I consent to act as secretary of the company named on page 1

Consent signature Signed Date

Directors *(See notes 1 - 5)*

Please list directors in alphabetical order.

Name

*Style/Title	CD
Forenames	
Surname	
*Honours etc	
Previous forenames	
Previous surname	

Address AD

Usual residential address must be given. In the case of a corporation, give the registered or principal office address.

Post town

County/Region

Postcode Country

Date of birth DO Nationality NA

Business occupation OC

Other directorships OD

* Voluntary details

I consent to act as director of the company named on page 1

Page 2 **Consent signature** Signed Date

Directors (continued)
(See notes 1 - 5)

Name	*Style/Title	CD
	Forenames	
	Surname	
	*Honours etc	
	Previous forenames	
	Previous surname	
Address		AD
Usual residential address must be given. In the case of a corporation, give the registered or principal office address.		
		Post town
		County/Region
		Postcode / Country
	Date of birth	DO / Nationality NA
	Business occupation	OC
	Other directorships	OD
* Voluntary details		I consent to act as director of the company named on page 1
	Consent signature	Signed / Date

Delete if the form is signed by the subscribers.

Signature of agent on behalf of all subscribers Date

Delete if the form is signed by an agent on behalf of all the subscribers.

All the subscribers must sign either personally or by a person or persons authorised to sign for them.

Signed	Date
Signed	Date
Signed	Date
Signed	Date
Signed	Date
Signed	Date

Page 3

Notes

1 Show for an individual the full forenames NOT INITIALS and surname together with any previous forenames or surname(s).

If the director or secretary is a corporation or Scottish firm - show the corporate or firm name on the surname line.

Give previous forenames or surname except that:

- for a married woman, the name by which she was known before marriage need not be given,
- names not used since the age of 18 or for at least 20 years need not be given.

In the case of a peer, or an individual usually known by a British title, you may state the title instead of or in addition to the forenames and surname and you need not give the name by which that person was known before he or she adopted the title or succeeded to it.

Address:

Give the usual residential address.

In the case of a corporation or Scottish firm give the registered or principal office.

2 Directors known by another description:

A director includes any person who occupies that position even if called by a different name, for example, governor, member of council. It also includes a shadow director.

3 Directors details:

Show for each individual director their date of birth, business occupation and nationality.
The date of birth must be given for every individual director.

4 Other directorships:

Give the name of every company of which the individual concerned is a director or has been a director at any time in the past 5 years. You may exclude a company which either **is** or at **all times during the past 5 years** when the person was a director **was**:

- dormant,
- a parent company which wholly owned the company making the return,
- a wholly owned subsidiary of the company making the return,
- another wholly owned subsidiary of the same parent company.

If there is insufficient space on the form for other directorships you may use a separate sheet of paper.

5 Use photocopies of page 2 to provide details of joint secretaries or additional directors and include the company's name.

6 The address for companies registered in England and Wales is:-

The Registrar of Companies
Companies House
Crown Way
Cardiff
CF4 3UZ

or, for companies registered in Scotland:-

The Registrar of Companies
Companies House
100-102 George Street
Edinburgh
EH2 3DJ

Figure 2: Companies Form 288

COMPANIES HOUSE

288

Change of director or secretary or change of particulars.

This form should be completed in black.

Company number CN

Company name

Appointment

(Turn over page for resignation and change of particulars).

	Day	Month	Year
Date of appointment DA			

Appointment of director CD

Appointment of secretary CS

Please mark the appropriate box. If appointment is as a director and secretary mark both boxes.

NOTES

Show the full forenames. **NOT INITIALS** If the director or secretary is a Corporation or Scottish firm, show the name on surname line and registered or principal office on the usual residential address line.

Give previous forenames or surname except:
- for a married woman the name before marriage need not be given.
- for names not used since the age of 18 or for at least 20 years.

A peer or individual known by a title may state the title instead of or in addition to the forenames and surname.

Name *Style/title

Forenames

Surname

*Honours etc

Previous forenames

Previous surname

Usual residential address AD

Post town

County/region

Postcode Country

Date of birth† DO Nationality† NA

Business occupation† OC

Other directorships†

Other directorships.

Give the name of every company incorporated in Great Britain of which the person concerned is a director or has been a director at any time in the past 5 years. Exclude a company which either is, or at all times during the past 5 years when the person was a director, was
- dormant
- a parent company which wholly owned the company making the return
- a wholly owned subsidiary of the company making the return
- another wholly owned subsidiary of the same parent company.

I consent to act as director/secretary of the above named company

Consent signature Signed Date

*Voluntary details †Directors only

A serving director etc must also sign the form overleaf.

Resignation

(This includes any form of ceasing to hold office e.g. death or removal from office).

Date of resignation etc — DR

Resignation etc, as director — XD

Resignation etc, as secretary — XS

Please mark the appropriate box. If resignation etc is as a director and secretary mark both boxes.

Forenames

Surname

Date of birth *(directors only)* — DO

If cessation is other than resignation, please state reason *(eg death)*

Change of particulars *(this section is not for appointments or resignations).*

Complete this section in all cases where particulars of a serving director/ secretary, have changed and then the appropriate section below.

Date of change of particulars — DC

Change of particulars, as director — ZD

Change of particulars, as secretary — ZS

Please mark the appropriate box. If change of particulars is as a director and secretary mark both boxes.

Forenames
Surname
(name previously notified to Companies House)

Date of birth *(directors only)* — DO

Change of name *(enter new name)* Forenames — NN

Surname

Change of usual residential address *(enter new address)* — AD

Post town

County/region

Postcode — Country

Other change *(please specify)*

A serving director,secretary etc must sign the form below.

Signature

Signed — Date

(by a serving director/secretary/administrator/ administrative receiver/receiver). *(Delete as appropriate)*

After signing please return the form to the Registrar of Companies at

Companies House, Crown Way, Cardiff CF4 3UZ
for companies registered in England and Wales

or **Companies House, 100-102 George Street, Edinburgh EH2 3DJ**
for companies registered in Scotland.

To whom should Companies House direct any enquiries about the information on this form?

Tel:

Board Meetings

There is no legal requirement to hold board meetings. Directors may regulate their proceedings as they think fit. The required quorum for a board meeting to do business is two, unless otherwise provided. Directors may act notwithstanding a vacancy in their number.

Larger companies normally hold board meetings monthly or fortnightly. Due notice must be given, and in default of such notice, the meeting will be irregular. The Articles may dispense with the notice requirement.

Where a meeting transacts business in spite of an irregularity caused by accidental omission, outsiders will not, generally, be prejudiced by such irregularity. This is known as the rule in *Royal British Bank v Turquand* (1856).

A board meeting may be held anywhere. Reasonable notice of the place must be given to all directors. It is a statutory requirement that minutes be kept of all board meetings. In particular, all decisions, and the reasons for reaching such decisions, should be carefully recorded. Failing to keep minutes is a criminal offence leading to a fine of £200 and a daily default fine of £20 for continued contravention.

Types of Director

Managing Director

The Articles of Association normally authorise the directors to delegate their functions to a managing director. The powers of a managing director depend upon the board and upon the terms of his service contract.

Shadow Director

A shadow director is a person who has not been formally appointed as a director, but who is nevertheless bound by most of the rules which cover ordinary directors. The condition for this is that the other directors must be accustomed to act in accordance with the directions or instructions of the shadow director.

Among the matters affecting shadow directors are the following.

- The duty to have regard to the interests of shareholders.
- The fact that shareholder approval must be obtained for directors' contracts of employment which are longer than five years.
- Restrictions on substantial property transactions.
- Controls over loans.
- The duty of disclosure of interests in contracts with the company.
- Prohibitions on dealing in share options.
- The duty of disclosure of shareholdings in a director's own company.
- Wrongful trading.
- Disqualification.

Checklist: Responsibilities of Shadow Directors

- Inclusion of personal details in register and business correspondence.
- Statutory rules dealing with accounts and annual returns.
- Reporting of transactions.
- Disclosure of interests.
- Duty to consider interests of employees.
- Approval of acquisition of assets.
- Reporting of acquisition or disposal of shares or debentures.
- Restrictions on loans.
- Wrongful trading.
- Disqualification.

Salaried Executive Director

This post is similar to that of managing director. Its terms will normally be set out in a service contract. In large public companies the board may consist of a number of non-executive directors who are paid for attending board meetings, plus full-time salaried directors who are described as executive directors and who are responsible for the day-to-day running of the company.

Alternate Directors

Table A provides that an alternate director, even where appointed to attend only one meeting in the absence of another director, is a director within the meaning of the Companies Act 1985. He is, therefore, subject to all the duties and responsibilities incurred by full-time directors.

Chairman

The function of the chairman is to act on behalf of all the members of the company present at meetings, and in particular as outlined below.

The Chairman's Function

- the regulation of business at meetings
- to close discussion when all points have been made
- to arrange votes
- to exercise a deciding vote if necessary
- to declare the results of polls
- the adjournment of meetings.

Remuneration

There is no automatic right for a director to be paid. Most directors will have a written contract with the company setting out the terms of their remuneration. It should be noted that loans by companies to directors are not, as a rule, allowed. (See Chapter 3.) The amount of payments to directors must be disclosed in the notes to the company accounts.

The question of whether remuneration is genuine was raised in *Re Halt Garage* (1982). The facts of that case were that in 1964 H acquired a ready-made company and carried on a garage business. He and his wife were the only directors. The company was empowered to pay remuneration to directors and to make a payment for the mere assumption of the post. In 1967 the wife fell ill and took no further part in the business. She continued to draw reduced remuneration until the company was wound up in 1971. H continued to draw remuneration throughout, despite the fact that in the last two years the company was insolvent. The liquidator brought proceedings claiming the whole of the wife's payments and that part of H's remuneration which exceeded the true value of his services.

The High Court stated that:

- Where payments are made to a director in pursuance of a company's powers to do so, the competence to award such payments depends upon whether they are genuinely director's remuneration and not a disguised capital gift. The court will not inquire as to whether they are reasonable.
- The payments to the wife were not for services rendered. They were ultra vires and could be recovered by the liquidator.

Contracts

Service Contracts

A service contract is essentially a document setting out terms of employment. It should deal with the following:

- the scope of duties and powers
- acceptance of decisions of the board
- commitment of the whole of the director's attention to the business of the company

- an obligation to treat information as confidential
- a promise not to compete with the company after ceasing to be director
- remuneration and benefits
- compensation for loss of office
- termination of contract
- duration of contract.

Copies of the contract must be held at the company's registered office or place of business. The terms of the contract must not be kept secret.

A service contract will normally amount to a contract of employment, and as such will be governed by the general principles of employment law. (See Chapter 6.) An example of a service contract is included at the end of this chapter.

Enforcement of Contracts on or After Termination of Employment

In the period up to departure from office and immediately afterwards, company directors have the following duties.

- To serve their employer/company honestly and faithfully during the period between severance and departure.
- To disclose any "moonlighting" profits if they derive from a contract the benefit of which rightfully belongs to the company.
- If a severance agreement is made with a director before he receives payment for "moonlighting" work, the severance payment is not recoverable on the grounds of unilateral mistake of fact. No mistake of fact can occur before the facts supporting it have occurred.
- There is no implied term in a director's service contract that he will not poach employees when he leaves. But such a clause may be expressly inserted into the contract.

These points are illustrated by the case of *Horcal Ltd v Gatland* (1983). H Ltd was a building company. G was managing director. He reached a preliminary agreement with W, a major shareholder, to buy H Ltd from W. In the light of this preliminary agreement G prepared an estimate for a customer. He did this on H Ltd notepaper but paid the cheque for the work into his own bank account. This was described as "moonlighting".

Subsequently W proposed a new agreement and offered G a golden handshake of £5000. This was accepted, and G left the company. W then discovered that G had been "moonlighting". He claimed repayment of the £5000 on the basis that if he had known of the moonlighting he would not have entered into the severance agreement. He argued that the agreement had been made as the result of a fundamental mistake and was totally void. W further complained that G had poached two employees on his departure in order to enable him to set up a competing business.

The Court of Appeal decided that the golden handshake money could not be recovered because it was paid to G before the profits from the "moonlighting". For the doctrine of mistake to operate in this context, the profit must have actually been made before the agreement which it is argued has been made void. In relation to poaching, W had no redress because there was no written term in the contract.

The case demonstrates that it is prudent practice to include in all severance agreements a clause stipulating that all matters, contracts, opportunities, etc have been disclosed to the company whether or not payment has been received, and that the severance agreement is absolutely subject to this complete disclosure.

Restrictive Covenants

The general rule is that whether or not a particular provision restricting a director's activities after termination of a directorship is valid, depends upon whether the employer has acted reasonably to protect his own legitimate interests.

In *Rex Stewart Jeffries Parker Ginsberg Ltd v Parker* (1988), P was employed as joint managing director of an advertising agency. His contract of service stated that the employment could be terminated "by the giving in writing of six calendar months' notice on either side or the payment of six months' salary in lieu thereof". In March 1986 P was told that he would be made redundant in a week's time and that he would receive six months' pay in lieu of notice.

After his dismissal P set up his own advertising agency. The former employers claimed an injunction to enforce a non-solicitation clause in his service contract. This clause prohibited him from soliciting clients for a period of 18 months after termination of his employment.

P argued that by dismissing him with one week's notice, the employers had been in fundamental breach of the contract of employment, so that he was no longer bound by the non-solicitation clause. Alternatively, he claimed that the clause was void as being unreasonable.

The Court of Appeal ruled that there had been no breach of contract: the contract itself had provided for payment in lieu of notice. Further, the period of 18 months was not in itself unreasonable.

The question of confidentiality was considered in *Lawrence David Ltd v Ashton* (1989). A was employed as sales director of a company which manufactured bodies for heavy goods vehicles. His contract of employment provided that he would not disclose any information or trade secrets during or after the termination of his employment. It also stated that for two years after the end of the contract he would not be employed in the same type of work.

A's contract was terminated and he was offered employment by one of his former employer's main competitors. The former employers sought an injunction to enforce the terms of A's contract.

The Court of Appeal ruled that the injunction would be granted, but it would not operate in respect of the term in the contract referring to information or trade secrets, because this was too vague.

The case of *Baker v Gibbons* (1972) gives further guidance on the meaning of "confidential information" in the context of restrictive covenants. B was a director of M

Co. which marketed its products through selling agents. The names of the agents were published in Yellow Pages, and in the course of his employment B obtained information as to their addresses and areas of operation. He made no written list. The agents were entitled to terminate their employment at any time. B was not subject to a restrictive covenant against competition on leaving the company.

The defendant directors of the company purported to remove B from office. He set up a competing business and solicited one of the selling agents to join him. The company sought an injunction to restrain B from soliciting its employees to terminate their employment.

The High Court refused to grant the injunction. It ruled that information as to the name and address of a particular employee of a company, obtained by a director during his tenure of office is not in itself to be regarded as having been received in confidence and remaining confidential.

Summary: Terms to be Included in Directors' Service Contracts

- Powers and duties to be delegated by Board.
- Duration of contract.
- Circumstances of termination of contract.
- Potential compensation for loss of office.
- Remuneration.
- Fringe benefits.
- Acceptance of authority of Board.
- Agreement to devote whole of time and attention to company's affairs.
- Confidentiality of company information.
- Restrictive covenant agreeing not to compete with company after termination.

An example of a service contract follows on the next page.

Example: Director's Service Contract

THIS **AGREEMENT** is made the day of 199[ ]

BETWEEN:

(1) [ ] whose registered office is at [ ]
("the Company");
AND
(2) [ ] of [ ]
("the Executive")

WHEREAS It is agreed as follows:

1. Appointment

1.1 The Company shall employ the Executive and the Executive shall serve the Company as its [ ] [or in such other capacity and to perform such other duties as the parties may from time to time agree].

1.2 Subject as hereinafter provided the Employment shall be for a fixed term of [ ] years commencing on [the date of this Agreement] and continuing thereafter unless and until terminated by not less than [ ] months written notice on either side expiring on or any time after the expiration of the fixed term.

[1.2 Subject as hereinafter provided the Employment of the Executive shall be deemed to have commenced on [ ] 199[ ] and shall continue subject to termination by either party giving to the other [ ] months' notice in writing.]

[1.2 Subject as hereinafter provided the Employment shall be for an initial period of one year from [ ] 199[ ] ("the Commencement Date") and on each anniversary of the Commencement Date shall be renewed for an additional year unless prior to the anniversary of the Commencement Date either party shall give to the other at least [one] month's notice in writing to expire on the last day before the anniversary of the Commencement Date].

1.3 The Company shall have the right to pay salary in lieu of notice (subject to deductions for tax and national insurance, if any).

2. Primary Duties

2.1 The Executive shall during his Employment:-

2.1.1 be responsible directly to [the Board];

2.1.2 be responsible for [the management of the Company] and shall additionally or alternatively undertake duties in relation to such other aspects of the Company's [and/or the Group's] business and affairs as [the Board] may from time to time determine but subject in every case to such restrictions as the Board may from time to time impose;

2.1.3 use his best endeavours to promote the interests of the Company [and the Group] and shall not engage in any activity which may be or become harmful to or contrary to the interests of the Company [or any member of the Group];

2.1.4 in the discharge of such duties and in the exercise of such powers observe and comply with all resolutions regulations and directions from time to time made or given by [the Board];

2.2 The Executive shall (subject only to Clause 3 below) devote the whole of his time and attention to the discharge of his duties hereunder in such place or places in [the United Kingdom and Eire] and abroad as [the Board] may from time to time [reasonably] direct and conform to such hours of work as [the Board] may reasonably require.

2.3 The Executive shall accept (if offered) appointment as a director of any member of the Group and from time to time as requested by the Board (but not otherwise) resign any such appointment without claim but so that such resignations shall not affect the continuance of the Employment.

3. Outside Interests

The Executive shall not without the consent of the Board during the continuance of the Employment be engaged or interested either directly or indirectly in any capacity in any trade business or occupation whatsoever other than the business of the Company [or the Group] but so that this provision shall not prohibit the holding whether directly or indirectly of shares or investments listed on a recognised stock exchange so long as not more than 3 per cent of the shares or stock of any class of any one company shall be so held.

4. Salary

4.1 Subject as hereinafter provided the Company shall pay to the Executive during the continuance of this Employment a salary [(subject to annual review on each year)] at the rate of £ per annum. The salary, which shall accrue from day to day, shall be deemed to include all or any sums receivable by the Executive as director's fees [from any member of the Group]. The salary shall be payable by equal monthly instalments in arrears on the last day of each month.

[4.2 An annual bonus may also be paid on terms and subject to conditions (determined from time to time by the Board) that have been notified to the Executive separately].

5. Expenses, Other Benefits [and Car]

5.1 The Executive shall be reimbursed, subject to the production of appropriate receipts or vouchers, all reasonable travelling hotel and other out of pocket expenses wholly necessarily and exclusively incurred by him in or about the discharge of his duties.

[5.2 The Company shall provide the Executive with a motor car of a type that [the Board] shall reasonably consider appropriate for the Executive having regard to the capacity in which he is employed hereunder for his use in or about the business of the Company during the Employment. The Executive shall also be permitted to use the motor car for his own private purposes, including use on holiday within the United Kingdom (and use by members of his family who are authorised in writing by the Company and are licensed to drive and insured for that purpose). The Company will pay all petrol [and other running costs] incurred by the Executive [on Company business] [whether incurred on Company business or during personal use]. The Executive shall at all times conform with all regulations which may from time to time be imposed by it with regard to motor cars provided by the Company for use by its officers or employees including regulations as to such personal use as aforesaid and payment therefore.]

[5.3 The Company shall provide membership for the Executive and his spouse and children (under 18) of [specify] private patients medical plan or with such medical expenses insurance scheme as the Company shall decide.]

6. Holidays

6.1 The Executive shall be entitled to [ ] working days holiday (and any public/Bank holidays) in each holiday year such days of holiday to be taken at such time or times as [the Board] shall agree. The Company's holiday year shall run from [1 January to 31 December]. The Executive [may] [may not] carry any unused part of his holiday entitlement to a subsequent holiday year or claim pay in lieu thereof [save that the Company may, in its discretion, allow the Executive to carry forward up to days holiday to [31 March] in the following year].

6.2 In the holiday year during which the Executive's Employment commences or terminates the Executive shall be entitled to such proportion of his annual holiday entitlement as the period of his Employment for each such year shall bear to one calendar year. Upon the termination of the Executive's Employment the Executive shall either be entitled to salary in lieu of any outstanding holiday entitlement or be required to repay (including by way of deduction from any monies which would otherwise be payable to the Executive upon the termination of this employment) to the Company any salary received in respect of holiday taken in excess of his proportionate holiday entitlement

7. Incapacity

7.1 If the Executive shall at any time be incapacitated or prevented by illness, injury, accident or any other circumstances beyond his control (such Incapacity or prevention being referred to below as "the Incapacity") from discharging his duties under this Agreement for a total of [ ] or more weeks in any twelve consecutive calendar months the Company may by notice in writing to the Executive given at any time so long as the Incapacity shall continue:-

7.1.1 discontinue payment in whole or in part of the salary payable under Clause 4.1 [and benefits payable under

Clause 5] above on or from such future date as may be specified in the notice until the Incapacity shall cease; or

7.1.2 (whether or not payment shall already have been discontinued as provided in 7.1.1 above) determine this Employment forthwith or on such future date as may be specified in the notice.

7.2 Subject as provided in 7.3 below salary (less any Statutory Sick Pay, Sickness Benefit or other National Insurance benefits receivable by the Executive) [and benefits] shall notwithstanding the Incapacity continue to be paid to the Executive in accordance with Clause[s] 4 [and 5] above in respect of the period of Incapacity prior to discontinuance or determination as provided in 7.1.1 above.

7.3 If the Incapacity shall be or appear to be occasioned by an actionable wrong of a third party in respect of which damages are or may be recoverable the Executive shall forthwith notify [the Board] of the fact and of that fact and of any claim, compromise, settlement or judgment made or awarded in connection therewith and shall give to [the Board] all such particulars of such matters as [the Board] may reasonably require and shall if so required by [the Board] may determine but not exceeding the amount of damages recovered by the Executive in respect of loss of remuneration under such compromise, settlement or judgment less any costs in or in connection with or under such claim, compromise, settlement or judgment borne by him and not exceeding the aggregate of the remuneration paid to him in respect of the period of the Incapacity.

7.4 The Executive agrees that at any reasonable time during his Employment he will undergo, if required by the Company, a medical examination by a medical practitioner appointed by the Company and at the Company's expense and that he will consent to such examination.

8. Pensions and Retirement

8.1 The Executive shall be entitled to become during his Employment a member of the [NAME] pension scheme subject to and in accordance with its terms and conditions as amended from time to time.

8.2 The Company shall be entitled to deduct from remuneration due to the Executive any contributions payable by him to any such scheme and to pay them to the trustees or administrator thereof.

8.3 A contracting out certificate [is/is not] in force in respect of the Executive's Employment.

8.4 The Executive shall retire automatically at the age of [ ] and no notice shall be required from the Company to terminate this Agreement at such age.

9. Confidential information

The Executive shall at all times during his Employment hereunder (and after the termination of his Employment howsoever arising without limit in point of time) keep secret (except to the extent that disclosure is authorised by the Company) all information which is of a confidential nature and of value to the Company or any member of the Group, including but without limitation:-

9.1 the business methods and information of the Company (including prices charged, discounts given to customers or obtained from suppliers, product development, marketing and advertising programmes, costings, budgets, turnover, sales targets or other financial information);

9.2 lists and particulars of the Company's [and/or any member of the Group's] suppliers and customers and the individual contacts at such suppliers and customers;

9.3 details and terms of the Company's and/or any member of the Group's agreements with suppliers and customers;

9.4 secret manufacturing or production processes and know-how employed by the Company and/or any member of the Group or its/their suppliers;

9.5 confidential details as to the design of the Company's and/or any member of the Group's or its and/or their suppliers' products and inventions or developments relating to future products;

whether or not in the case of documents they are or were marked as confidential. This restriction shall cease to apply to information or knowledge which shall come (otherwise than by breach of this Clause) into the public domain

10. Restrictive covenants

10.1 The Executive acknowledges that he has, in the course of his Employment, acquired confidential information, trade secrets and knowledge about the business, operations, clients and connections of the Company and agrees to enter into the restrictions in this Clause for the purpose of protecting those interests of the Company [and/or Group companies].

10.2 The Executive shall not for a period of [ ] months after the termination of his Employment, howsoever arising, directly or indirectly, on his own behalf, or on behalf of any person, firm or company:-

10.2.1 solicit or canvass the custom of any person, firm or company who during the [12] months prior to the termination of his Employment was a customer or potential customer of the Company [and/or any other member of the Group] and (in the case of a customer) from whom he had obtained business or to whom he had provided services on behalf of the Company [and/or any other member of the Group] or (in the case of a potential customer) with whom he had dealt with a view to obtaining business;

10.2.2 deal with any person, firm or company who during the [12] months prior to the termination of his Employment was a customer or potential customer of the Company [and/or any other member of the Group] and (in the case of a customer) from whom he had obtained business or to whom he had provided services on behalf of the Company [and/or any other member of the Group] or (in the case of a potential customer) with whom he had dealt with a view to obtaining business;

10.2.3 within [RESTRICTED AREA] set up, carry on, be employed in, provide services to, be associated with, or be engaged or interested in, whether as director, employee, principal, agent or otherwise howsoever [save as a shareholder of not more than 3% of any public company whose shares are quoted on any recognised Stock Exchange] any business which is or is intended or about to be similar to or competitive with any type of business carried on by the Company at the date of termination of Employment of the Executive and with which the Executive was concerned at any time during the 12 months immediately preceding the termination of his Employment;

10.2.4 employ, or offer to employ, or attempt to employ, or entice away, or enter into partnership with, or attempt to enter into partnership with, any employee of the Company [or the Group] who was employed by the Company [or the Group] at the time of the termination of the Executive's Employment;

10.3 The restrictions contained in this Clause 10 are considered by the parties to be reasonable in all the circumstances. It is agreed that if any one or more of the restrictions shall either be taken by itself or by themselves to go beyond what is reasonable in all the circumstances for the protection of the interests of the Company [and/or Group] but would be considered reasonable if any particular restriction or restrictions were deleted or any part or parts of the wording in the restriction or restrictions were deleted or limited in any particular way then the restriction shall apply with such deletions or limitations.

11. Designs and Inventions

11.1 All designs, inventions, programmes, discoveries or improvements ("Designs and Inventions") conceived apprehended or learned by the Executive during the course of or arising out of his Employment (whether alone or together with any other person or persons) and which concern or are applicable to products or articles manufactured or sold by or to services provided by the Company [and/or any member of the Group] shall be the exclusive property of the Company.

11.2 Any such Designs and Inventions shall be disclosed to the Company whether conceived, apprehended or learned by the Executive during the course of or after termination of his Employment (howsoever such termination may occur)

11.3 The Executive shall at all times whether during the course of or after the termination of his Employment (howsoever such termination may occur):-

11.3.1 not without the prior written consent of the Company apply for any patent or design registration as the case may be either in the United Kingdom or in any other part of the world for any such Design or Invention so conceived or made by him;

11.3.2 if and whenever required by the Company to do so (and in such manner as the Company shall in its sole discretion decide) apply as a nominee of or jointly with the Company for patent or design registration in the United Kingdom and as the Company may require any other part of the world for any such Design or Invention so conceived or made by him and shall sign all such documents and do all such things as may be necessary effectively to vest all applications at any time and from time to time pending and all resulting patents and design registration when granted and all right title and interest to and in the same in the Company absolutely as sole beneficial owner or as the Company may require;

11.3.3 upon demand by the Company sign all such documents execute all such deeds and do all such things as may be necessary for the purpose of obtaining patent or design registration for any such Designs or Inventions in any country in the world and for effectively vesting all and any such patents and design registration in the Company as sole beneficial owner or as the Company may require.

11.4 The Executive hereby irrevocably appoints and authorises the Company to act as his attorney and agent for the purposes of executing and/or signing all or any such documents as may be required to give the Company (and/or its nominee and/or assignee) the full benefit of the provisions of this Clause.

11.5 The Company shall pay all expenses in connection with any application for patent or design registration made by the Executive as nominee for or jointly with the Company pursuant to this Clause.

11.6 The Company shall hold the Executive indemnified against all liabilities to third parties in connection with or arising out of all and any applications and all and any resulting patents and design registrations which may be granted if and to the extent that any such liabilities arise from the act or default of the Company.

11.7 It shall be presumed (but subject to proof to the contrary) that the subject matter of any application for a patent or design registration filed by the Executive or any assignee or agent of the Executive within 12 months after the termination of his Employment (howsoever such termination may arise) and relating to goods or services of a kind with which the Executive was concerned in the course of his duties at any time during the currency of his Employment is a Design or Invention made by the Executive during the currency of his Employment.

12. Summary Termination

12.1 The Executive's Employment under this Agreement may be terminated forthwith by the Company without prior notice if the Executive shall at any time:-

(a) commit any serious breach or repeat after warning any breach of any of the provisions of this Agreement; or

(b) be guilty of any serious misconduct or (after warning) wilful neglect in the discharge of his duties under this Agreement; or

(c) be adjudicated bankrupt or make any arrangement or composition with his creditors; or

(d) become of unsound mind or if while he is a patient within the meaning of Part VII of the Mental Health Act 1983 an order shall be made in respect of his property under Section 95 of that Act or any statutory modification or re-enactment thereof; or

(e) be convicted of any criminal offence (other than minor offenses under the Road Traffic Acts and the Road Safety Acts) which in the reasonable opinion of the Board materially adversely affects his ability to continue in office as an employee or officer of the Company (including bringing himself or the Company into disrepute)

12.2 On termination under Clause 12.1 the Company shall not be obliged to make any further payment to the Executive beyond the amount of any remuneration actually accrued due to the date of such termination and the Company shall be entitled to deduct from such remuneration any sums owing to the Company [or any other member of the Group] by the Executive.

13. Termination Generally

13.1 Upon the termination of this Employment for whatsoever reason:-

13.1.1 the Executive shall upon the request of the Company resign from all (if any) offices held by him in the Company or any member of the Group and all (if any) trusteeships held by him of any pension scheme or other trust established or subscribed to/by any member of the Group and in the event of his failure to do so the Company is hereby irrevocably authorised to appoint some person in his name and on his behalf to execute any documents and do all things requisite to give effect to such resignations;

13.1.2 deliver up to the Company all correspondence, drawings, documents and other papers and all other property belonging to the Company or any member of the Group (including to car specified in Clause 5) which may be in the Executive's possession or under his control;

13.1.3 if so requested send to the Company secretary a signed statement confirming that he has complied with sub-Clause 13.1.2 hereof.

[13.2 the Company shall have no liability to the Executive for the effect of such termination on any agreement between the Executive and any other member of the Group or on any option right or privilege granted to the Executive by the Company or other member of the Group].

13.3 The Executive shall not at any time after the termination of his Employment, howsoever arising, represent himself as being in any way connected with or interested in the business of the Company or any member of the Group.

14. Novation

14.1 In the event of this Employment being terminated in connection with any scheme of reconstruction or amalgamation and the Executive being offered employment with another company thereunder on terms substantially not less favourable to the Executive than the terms of this Agreement the Executive shall have no claim against the Company by reason of such termination.

14.2 If the Executive shall at any time have been offered but shall have unreasonably refused or failed to agree to the transfer of this Agreement by way of novation to the Company which has acquired or agreed to acquire the whole or substantially the whole of the undertaking and assets or not less than fifty per cent of the equity share capital of the Company the Executive shall have no claim against the Company by reason of the termination of his Employment by the Company on one month's notice to the Executive given within one month of such offer.

15. Notices

Notices may be given by either party by letter or telefacsimile message addressed to the other party at (in the case of the Company) its registered office for the time being and (in the case of the Executive) his last known address and any such notice given by letter shall be deemed to have been given at the time at which the letter would be delivered in the ordinary course of post.

16. Definitions and Interpretation

16.1 In this Agreement:-

"Board" means board of directors of the Company from time to time;

"Employment" means the employment under this Agreement;

"Group" means the Company and all companies which are for the time being either a holding company of the Company or a subsidiary or associated company of either the Company or any such holding company; "subsidiary company" and "holding company" have the meanings ascribed to them by Section 736 of the Companies Act 1985 or any statutory modification or re-enactment thereof;

"associated company" in relation to a company means any company in which that company or any holding company of it is directly or indirectly beneficially interested in ten per cent or more of the relevant company's issued ordinary share capital.

16.2 This Agreement shall be read and construed without reference to its Clause headings which are included for convenience only.

17. Termination of Prior Agreements

This Agreement is in substitution for all previous contracts of service between the Company [and/or the Group] and the Executive such agreements shall be deemed to have been terminated by mutual consent as from the date on which this Agreement takes effect.

18. Statutory Particulars

Notice is hereby given to the Executive under the provisions of the Employment Protection (Consolidation) Act 1978 as follows:-

18.1 The Executive's date of commencement of continuous employment (including any previous employment counting for this purpose) was [ ] 19[];

18.2 any grievance which the Executive may have in relation to this Employment shall be expressed in writing to the Secretary or Chairman of the Company (to whom he should also apply if dissatisfied with any disciplinary decision) and shall be referred to the Board for decision;

18.3 In the event of an alleged breach pursuant to Clause 12(a) or (e) a disciplinary hearing will be held by a nominated member of the Board [OR SET OUT SUCH RULES AS THERE MAY BE OR REFER TO ANY DOCUMENT CONTAINING SUCH RULES].

19. English Law

This Agreement shall be construed and governed by English Law and the parties submit to the non-exclusive jurisdiction of the English Courts.

IN WITNESS whereof this Agreement has been executed as a deed by the parties hereto the day and year first above written

SIGNED and delivered)
as a deed by)
[NAME OF COMPANY])
in the presence of :-)

[Director]

[Secretary]

SIGNED and delivered)
as a deed by the said)
[NAME OF EMPLOYEE])
in the presence of :-)

3 Directors' Duties

The directors are the persons with primary responsibility for the running of a company. The Articles will normally state the extent of their authorisation to manage the company's affairs. Article 70 of Table A allows directors to exercise all powers which are not expressly reserved to the shareholders' general meeting.

> **Summary: Director's Day-to-Day Management Duties**
>
> - Preparation of accounts
> - Drafting annual directors' reports
> - Supplying auditors with information
> - Calling general meetings
> - Appointing company secretary
> - Engaging auditors

ACCOUNTS

The main aim of imposing a duty upon companies to provide financial information in their annual accounts is to ensure that shareholders can exercise their rights. The general duties of directors in relation to company accounts are:

- ensuring that the company's transactions are sufficiently recorded
- preparing and approving annual accounts
- supervising the sending of the annual accounts, auditors' report and directors' report to all shareholders
- supplying the above documents to the shareholders in general meeting

- delivering the documents to the registrar of companies within the permitted period

Accounts must be very carefully prepared so as to give a "true and fair view" of the company's financial position. The statutory rules are detailed and complex and it is the duty of every director to abide by them. Although day-to-day details of accounting procedures may be delegated to a financial director, general collective responsibility remains with all the directors.

By statute, every company must keep the following accounting records

- entries from day to day of all sums of money received and expended by the company and the matters in respect of which the receipt and expenditure takes place
- records of the assets and liabilities of the company
- if the company deals in goods:
  - statements of all stockholdings and (except for retail businesses) of all goods sold and purchased so as to enable the identification of buyers and sellers
  - statements of stock held by the company at the end of each financial year.

These records must be adequate to explain transactions entered into by the company and to disclose the financial position of the company. They must also enable the directors to ensure that the balance sheet or profit and loss account gives a true and fair view.

Records must be stored at the company's registered office or such other place as the directors decide and be available for inspection by officers of the company. They must be preserved for three years in the case of a private company and six for a public company.

Duty to Prepare Accounts

It is the duty of the directors to prepare a profit and loss account and a balance sheet as at the last day of the financial year. The balance sheet must be signed by a director on behalf of the board. These are known as the individual accounts. In relation to groups of companies, the directors must prepare group accounts. These accounts, together with the directors' report, must be sent to the members of the company, laid before the company in general meeting and delivered to the Registrar of Companies.

The financial year, for these purposes, depends on the accounting reference period. This is determined by the accounting reference date. A company may decide its own accounting reference date: if it does not, it will be deemed to be a specified date according to statutory rules. The main significance of this for directors is that the accounts must be laid before the general meeting and delivered to the Registrar within 10 months of the accounting reference date for private companies, and within seven months for public.

Directors' Report

This must contain the following information:

- A review of the company's business during the financial year.
- Amounts of dividends.
- Names of directors.
- The main activities of the company.
- Changes in company assets.
- Changes in market value of land.
- Interests of directors in shares of the company.
- A statement of important events affecting the company.
- Information as to disabled employees and the scope of employee involvement and participation in the company.
- Certain specified information in relation to the purchase of shares in the company.
- Details of amounts spent for political or charitable purposes.

Penalties

The Companies Act 1985 sets out criminal penalties for breach of the accounting requirements. On trial on indictment the directors are liable to an unlimited fine. The penalty for summary conviction is a maximum fine of £2000. It is a defence for a director to be able to show that he has acted honestly and that the default was reasonable in the circumstances.

On average, 160 directors are prosecuted each month for offences in relation to accounting requirements. In 1991, 3356 directors faced criminal charges of failing to file annual returns, and 1864 were prosecuted for not filing annual accounts. Conviction means a criminal record. The current attitude of Companies House is reported to be much tougher than in the past.

From 1 July 1992 directors filing late accounts will receive an automatic fine of a maximum of £5000 for a public company and £1000 for a private. Failure to comply with responsibilities to prepare accounts may also be a ground for disqualification (see Chapter 5).

Auditors

An auditor must be appointed either by the directors or by the shareholders before the first general meeting at which the accounts are submitted. A director is prohibited from being an auditor.

The main function of the auditor is to report to the shareholders as to whether the accounts have been properly prepared and give a true and fair account of the financial position of the company. He is not responsible for preparing the accounts–this remains the responsibility of the directors.

Exemptions from Accounting Requirements

Special rules apply to small and medium-sized companies. These are defined as follows:

Small company:
Turnover under £2 million
Balance sheet total under £975,000

Average number of employees not exceeding 50

Medium-sized company:
Turnover under £8 million
Balance sheet total under £3,900,000
Average number of employees not exceeding 250

A small or medium-sized company which is not a public company, a banking, insurance or shipping company, nor an authorised person under the Financial Services Act 1986, may deliver modified accounts. These comprise:

Small company:
Directors' report: not required
Profit and loss account: not required
Balance sheet in modified form
Source and application of funds statement: not required

Medium sized-company:
Profit and loss account may be filed in modified form
Disclosure and analysis of turnover: not required
Source and application of funds statement: not required

Where directors file modified accounts they must include a statement that they have relied upon the exemptions, together with a special auditors' report confirming the figures.

Dormant Companies

These are defined by section 250 of the 1985 Act as follows:

- It is a small company, as defined above.
- It has been dormant since its formation, if no accounts have yet been laid, or since the end of its last financial year.
- It has entered into no significant accounting transactions during the current year.

Such a company is entitled to the small company exemptions even if it is part of a group of companies which makes it otherwise ineligible.

Cadbury Committee Recommendations

The Cadbury Report on the financial aspects of corporate

governance has recommended that the Companies Act 1985 should be amended to release auditors from their duty of confidentiality to companies. The Report proposes that auditors should be free to report reasonable suspicions of fraud.

The Cadbury Committee was set up to consider the responsibilities of directors in relation to accounting matters. In addition to its proposals on auditors, it has made the following recommendations.

- The board should meet regularly, retain full control over the company and report on executive management.
- Responsibilities at the head of the company should be divided.
- A balance of authority should be achieved, so that no single individual has unfettered power.
- If the chairman of the board is also the chief executive, then there should be a strong independent element on the board.
- There should be sufficient non-executive directors to ensure that their views carry weight in the board's decisions. The role of the non-executive director should be to bring independent judgement to bear upon long-term strategy.
- Non-executive directors should be appointed for fixed terms, without automatic re-appointment.

Duty to Act Bona Fide

This duty involves consideration of the shareholders' interests. But when a company is in financial difficulties, then the interests of creditors must also be considered. In *Brady v Brady* (1987) it was said that even where a company is doubtfully solvent the interests of the company are really the interests of existing creditors alone.

Another example of the application of the principle is *Re Roith* (1967) where the controlling director of a company was aged 58 and no longer in good health. He consulted solicitors about providing for his wife and keeping the company going after his death. As a result, the company's articles were amended to allow the provision of pensions and he was given, for the first time, a service agreement which provided for payment to his executors of a pension in trust for his wife.

Five years after he died the company went into liquidation. The widow claimed for the capitalised value of her pension. The court held that in all the circumstances the pension had not been reasonably incidental to the carrying on of the company's business nor entered into bona fide for the benefit of, and to promote the prosperity of, the company. Her claim was rejected.

The early dealings of Robert Maxwell have also contributed to the "interests of the company" rule. In *Pergamon Press v Maxwell* (1970), P Inc was an American company of which 70% of the shares was owned by P of England. M was president of P Inc, chairman and managing director of P, and controlled 34% of the shares in P. It was a rule of P Inc that special meetings of the shareholders could be called at the request of the majority of shareholders entitled to vote at such meetings.

In June 1969 M, having general power to do so, voted for new rules repealing that right, and retaining it for himself. The new rules were passed. Subsequently P Inc acquired 38% of the shares in P. M and other directors were removed from office in P, but refused to resign from P Inc. P had no means of calling a meeting to remove them. P sought in the English court an order that M should call a meeting of P Inc.

The English High Court decided that it could not interfere with the exercise of a director's fiduciary powers arising from the management of a foreign company. The power to convene a meeting was a discretionary power which M was bound to exercise in good faith in the interest of P Inc as a whole. The court of New York was the only proper tribunal in which the members of P Inc could seek to control its exercise.

Duty to Act for Proper Purposes

Directors' powers must not be exercised for any "collateral

purpose". This means that their conduct may be challenged if they act in a way which the Articles did not intend them to. For example, in *Hogg v Cramphorn Ltd* (1967) the directors allotted shares to people who they believed would support them in their office. They acted in the belief that their actions were in the best interests of the company. The court decided that they had used their power of allotment for a purpose which had not been intended by the Articles and the allotments were voidable.

A procedural point in connection with this principle arose in *Re A Company* (1986). The facts were that a large country house had been converted into flats. The freehold was owned by a management company in which each flat owner held one share. The company wished to introduce a new arrangement whereby shares were allotted according to contributions to the service charge. One shareholder alleged that this proposal concealed a sinister motive and that the directors were not acting for proper purposes. He sought an advance order indemnifying himself for costs. The court stated that there was no entitlement to such an order.

Other Duties

Trusteeship

A director is a trustee of company assets under his control. This means that he is personally answerable for the misapplication of such assets. "Misapplication" in this context means an unauthorised disposal or a transaction carried out other than in accordance with the duty to act bona fide in the interests of the company. For example, where a director makes a valuable technical discovery in the course of his company duties he holds that discovery on trust for the company.

In *Cook v Deeks* (1916) directors took advantage, for their own personal benefit, of an opportunity to make a contract. The opportunity arose only because they were directors, and would have been of considerable benefit to the company. The court ruled that they were liable to repay to the company profits which they had made from the contract.

Agency

Directors are agents of their company which means that the legal rules concerning principal and agent operate in relation to directors. Wherever an agent would be liable, so are directors: where the principal would be liable, then liability attaches to the company.

Wrongful Trading

See Chapter 4.

Disclosure of Interests

Any director who has an interest in any contract, transaction or arrangement with the company must declare the nature of his interest to the other directors. See also Substantial Property Transactions; Loans; later in this Chapter.

A recent example of this is *Guinness v Saunders* (1988) where X Co was taken over by Y Co. The takeover was effected by a directors' committee of which Z was a member. During the takeover, Y Co paid £5 million to a company controlled by Z for his services in effecting the takeover. Z stated that he had disclosed his interest in the company to the directors' committee.

The Court of Appeal ruled that a director with an interest in a contract with the company must disclose it to the whole board and not just to a directors' committee. Failure to do so will result in him becoming a constructive trustee of the benefits transferred.

Interests in Shares and Debentures

Directors are obliged to notify their interests in shares or debentures of the company. This includes changes in those interests. The interests of the directors' families are deemed to be those of the directors, although there are a number of exceptions to this rule. Every company must keep a register of directors' interests in shares and debentures.

Summary: Directors' Duties of Disclosure

Information to be kept at registered office:

- Christian name, surname and initials, and previous names
- Address
- Occupation
- Share or other financial interest in company

Disclosures in accounts:

- Interest in contract or proposed contract with company
- Loans by company

Conflict of Interest

The general rule is that directors should not put themselves in a position which is likely to cause a conflict of interest between their own interests, or those of a third party, and those of their company. For example, a director employed by one company cannot, in principle, act as director of another, because this would cause a potential conflict of interest.

The question of competing interests was considered in *Balston v Headline Filters* (1990) where it was stated that an intention by a director to set up in competition with the company after his directorship has come to an end is not a breach of fiduciary duty through conflict of interest.

The principle is also illustrated by *Lindgren v L & P Estates* (1968) where the plaintiffs were trustees of a settlement for the children of the chairman of a public company, of which the first plaintiff was also a director. The owner of the defendant company agreed to sell his shares to the public company, the transfer to be completed on 20 March 1968, and consented to the defendant company entering into an agreement with the plaintiff trustees for the grant to them of a lease of part of the property. This agreement was exchanged with the plaintiffs immediately after the share purchase took effect. The agreement, made by the defendant company's two directors on its behalf, was never completed by deed but possession was given to the plaintiffs and the agreement's provisions were acted upon until 1963. The plaintiffs then required the defendant company to complete the agreement by executing the lease.

The defendant company refused to do so on the ground that the agreement was void or voidable because it had been made by its two directors in breach of their duty, at the instance of two "directors-elect" who also acted in breach of duty. The plaintiffs obtained a decree of specific performance. The defendants appealed.

The Court of Appeal decided the following:

- There was no evidence that the defendant company's directors had been in breach of duty.
- Even if there had been such a breach, it would not have availed the defendant company because the directors had been affirmed in their position after the defendant company had knowledge of the material facts.
- The chairman of the public company and the first plaintiff, although prospective directors when the defendant company made the agreement, owed it no duty at that time as "directors-elect", nor was a director of a parent company debarred from contracting with a subsidiary company with an independent board.
- The decree of specific performance should be granted.

Thus the main points which emerged from the decision were:

- No duty is owed to a company by a prospective director before his appointment becomes effective.
- A director of a parent company is not debarred from contracting with a subsidiary which has an independent board of directors.

Fraudulent Trading

It is a criminal offence for a director to be involved in trading by a company to defraud creditors. If it appears that company business has been carried on for a fraudulent purpose, then on the application of the liquidator, the court may order those involved to make a contribution to the company's assets. The prosecution must prove dishonesty and an intention to defraud. This is established on proof of an intention dishonestly to prejudice the creditors in receiving payment of their debts.

A recent example is *Re A Company* (1990). A company had exceeded its overdraft limit, was in arrears of tax payments and had not paid its trade creditors. It continued to pay remuneration to the managing director. The company went into voluntary liquidation. The liquidator brought proceedings for fraudulent trading. The court ordered the managing director to pay £150,000 for the company's debts and liabilities.

In *Re Todd* (1990) a director was convicted of fraudulent evasion of liability to pay VAT. This amounted to carrying on the business of the company with intent to defraud creditors. The decision of the court was that defrauding the Commissioners of Customs and Excise and failing to make PAYE deductions were matters of real moral blame according to the current notions of fair trading among commercial men.

Again, in *Re Augustus Barnett & Son* (1986), AB was a subsidiary of R, a Spanish company with interests in wine and sherry production. AB had a deficiency of current assets. Its auditors refused to certify its accounts unless R certified that it would continue to support AB. Between June 1982 and June 1983 R gave a number of assurances that it would support AB. In September 1983 AB went into voluntary liquidation.

The liquidator sought a declaration that R was guilty of fraudulent trading in that it had knowingly been a party to carrying on the business of AB with intent to defraud creditors. He alleged that R had induced AB to continue to trade, had induced creditors and suppliers to continue to do business with AB, and had no intention of honouring its assurances. R applied to strike out the application. The High Court allowed R's application on the ground that there was no evidence of intention to defraud.

Property Transactions

"Substantial property transactions" involving a director, or persons connected with him, are restricted by law. The general rule is that such a transaction is prohibited unless:

- it is approved in advance by the shareholders in general meeting
- it is affirmed by the shareholders within a reasonable period
- the value of the property is less than £2000 or, if greater, the lesser of 10% of the company's assets or £100,000
- the transaction is between a wholly owned subsidiary and its holding company or a fellow wholly owned subsidiary
- it is with a company in the course of being wound up
- the acquisition of the asset is being acquired by a director in his capacity as a member.

If these rules are not complied with, then the company may treat the transaction as void unless the property can no longer be restored to the company or a third party has bona fide given value to acquire the property. The director may also be held personally liable to the company for any loss suffered.

Loans

A contract for a loan, quasi-loan or credit transaction of more than £5000 by a company to a director or to a person connected with him is, in general, voidable. A company or a director involved in the transaction is guilty of a criminal offence. A "loan" has been defined as a sum of money lent for a time to be returned in money or money's worth. This can include excessive or unspent claims for expenses.

A "quasi-loan" means a transaction by which the company meets a director's financial obligations on condition that the company will be reimbursed at a later date.

"Connected person" means the following:

- spouse
- children
- associated company
- a trustee where the person to whom the loan is made is a beneficiary of that trust
- partners.

Criminal penalties and civil remedies for breaches of these rules include the following:

- It is a criminal offence to knowingly authorise or permit such a transaction.
- A director or connected person who benefits from such a transaction must repay the company any profit made from it, and indemnify the company against any losses.

Personal Profits

It is a strict rule that a director should not keep personal profits which he would not have made if he had not been a director. An example of the application of this rule is *Industrial Development Corporation v Cooley* (1972). A was employed as managing director by B who provided construction consultancy services for gas boards. C, a gas board, offered a lucrative contract which B was keen to obtain. C told A that B would not get the contract because C disapproved of its organisation. A therefore told B that he was ill and terminated his employment with B on short notice. While he was still an employee of B he took steps which resulted in him obtaining the contract for himself. B sued A for an account of profits.

The High Court ruled that the fact that B could not have obtained the contract was immaterial. A had acted in breach of duty and must account. The rule is that a person who in the course of his employment obtains a contract for himself, is liable to account to his employer for the profit he makes, even if it can be shown that the employer would never have obtained the contract.

Secret Profits

The main case in this area is *Regal (Hastings) Ltd v Gulliver* (1942). The facts were that directors who honestly made a profit through buying and selling the company's own shares were held liable to repay the profit. This principle may now be excluded by the Articles, but it probably still applies where a director makes a profit through dealing with the company's shares on the basis of confidential information.

A more recent example is that of *Guinness v Saunders*

(No. 2) where X was a director of Guinness when it made a take-over bid for Distillers. X received a payment of £5.2 million for his services in connection with the bid. This was not diclosed at a directors' meeting. Guinness claimed that the money should be repaid. The High Court ruled that a director who fails to disclose his interest in a contract to a directors' meeting holds his "secret profit" on trust for the company. It must be repaid. The rule on secret profits is of less significance since the introduction of a statutory prohibition on insider dealing (see below).

Option Dealings

It is unlawful for a director or his family to buy or sell options in the company's shares or debentures. This prohibition applies to subsidiary companies but extends only to securities listed on a Stock Exchange.

Insider Dealing

Insider dealing is the use of confidential information relating to securities which is used by the person holding it to make a profit. The Company Securities (Insider Dealing) Act 1985 makes it a criminal offence to deal in securities in relation to which a person has information which it would be reasonable for him not to disclose, and which is "unpublished price sensitive information". This means that the offence can be committed in three possible ways:

- By dealing as an insider.
- By counselling or procuring insider dealing.
- By communicating unpublished price sensitive information. "Unpublished price sensitive information" means information about a company which is not generally known to outsiders and which would be likely to materially affect the price of that company's securities.

The offence relates to "persons connected with the company". This means the following:

- directors
- officers or employees with access to unpublished price-sensitive information

- persons with a business or professional relationship with the company which gives them access to such information
- persons connected with a subsidiary or holding company of the company in question
- "tippees", persons who obtain inside information from someone who was connected with the company during the previous six months.

In Attorney-General's Reference: No. 1 of 1988, an employee was held to have committed an offence where he had not made efforts to acquire price sensitive information, but had had it communicated to him, and had then purchased shares in the relevant company.

Duties to Shareholders

The shareholders are the owners of the company. They exercise their powers in general meetings. An annual general meeting (AGM) must be held every year. The directors are responsible in criminal law for failure to call an AGM.

An *extraordinary* general meeting (EGM) must be called in the following circumstances:

- where the holders of at least 10% of the share capital requisition an EGM
- under the terms of a court order
- where the assets of the company fall to less than half the value of its share capital. Any director who knowingly and wilfully fails to call the EGM in these circumstances is guilty of a criminal offence.

Periods of notice to be given for shareholders' meetings are prescribed by statute. There is no legal requirementf or directors to be present at meetings, but they should all attend the AGM to account for their running of the company.

Duty and Standard of Skill and Care

A recent general statement on the scope of this duty was made in the case of *Dorchester Finance Co v Stebbings* (1989). The directors of a company must act in good faith and in the interests of the company. They must also display such skill as can reasonably be expected of persons with their knowledge and experience and at all times must take such care as a prudent man would take on his own behalf.

The facts of the case were that non-executive directors had signed blank cheques: the court stated that no distinction was to be drawn between executive and non-executive directors in relation to the general standard of skill and care.

In *Re City Equitable Insurance* (1925) the following rules were stated:

- There is no duty upon a director to exhibit a greater degree of skill than may be reasonably expected from a person of his knowledge and experience.
- A director is not bound to give continuous attention to the affairs of the company.
- Reasonable delegation of powers and responsibilities is acceptable.

The significance of these rules is as follows:

- A director is not assumed to be an expert unless he is appointed as such. In *Re Brazilian Rubber Plantations & Estates Ltd* (1911) it was stated that a director is expected to act with such care as is reasonably to be expected from him, having regard to his knowledge and experience. He is not bound to bring any special qualifications to his office. In relation to the rubber industry, for example, he may take on the management of a rubber company in ignorance of anything connected with rubber. In such circumstances he will not be liable for mistakes resulting from such ignorance. But if he knows the rubber business then he must give the company the benefit of his experience.

- Directors are not liable for errors of judgement. If they act within their powers, with such care as is reasonably expected from them, having regard to their knowledge and experience, and if they act honestly for the benefit of the company, then they discharge their duties. In appropriate circumstances, they may obtain outside expert advice. In some cases, indeed, they may be liable for not obtaining such advice.

- A director may place reasonable reliance upon co-directors and other officers of the company. In *Dovey v Cory* (1901) a bank sustained heavy losses through the issue of fraudulent balance sheets and the advancing of improper loans. These frauds had been carried out by the manager and the chairman. The issue in the case was whether an innocent co-director could be liable for negligence in not having uncovered the frauds. The House of Lords decided that he was not liable on the basis that he had properly delegated the details of management. It could not be expected of a director that he should be watching either the inferior officers of the bank or verifying the calculations of the auditor. Business could not go on if people could not trust subordinates whose express work was attention to detail. The innocent co-director was entitled to rely upon the judgement, information and advice of the chairman and general manager, as to whose integrity, skill and competence he had no reason for suspicion.
- Continuous non-attendance at board meetings may amount to negligence. In *Re Perry* (1876) it was stated that a director is not bound to attend every meeting. Even where a director has been found to be negligent by non-attendance at meetings, it may be impossible to show that this has caused loss to the company.

In *Norman v Theodore Goddard* (1992) it was stated that it was not a breach of a fiduciary duty for a director to invest monies belonging to the company in an Isle of Man company, on the basis of advice given by a solicitor experienced in trusts and tax law.

Mr Justice Hoffman ruled that the correct test of a director's duty was that set out in section 214 (4) of the Insolvency Act 1986. The director in question was a chartered surveyor who had been persuaded to become a director of a property management company. The legal position was that he was expected to exercise reasonable skill in property management, but not in offshore tax avoidance. He had acted reasonably in relying on the advice of a solicitor experienced in corporate trusts and tax work. The solicitor was a man in a position of trust upon whom a director could reasonably be expected to rely.

It is important to note that these principles may be displaced by express terms in a director's service contract which may impose a responsibility for him to devote the whole of his working time to the company's affairs.

Investigations

The Department of Trade and Industry (DTI) has wide powers to order the investigation of a company's affairs or its ownership and control. The investigation will result in a written report, which may have the following consequences:

- Prosecution for criminal offences which have come to light during the investigation.
- An application for a disqualification order (see Chapter 5).
- A petition for the company to be wound up
- Civil proceedings for the recovery of property, where the DTI decides that such proceedings should be brought in the public interest. A number of recent cases have been heard concerning the rights and duties of directors during investigations by liquidators or by the DTI.

Self-Incrimination

In *Bishopsgate Investment Management v Maxwell* (1992) the Court of Appeal ruled that a company director could not rely upon the privilege against self-incrimination in refusing to give information to provisional liquidators. The Court stated that the aim of the Insolvency Act 1986 was to promote harmony between the systems of personal and company insolvency. Each system had provided for public examination in court, and for private examination. The 1986 Act had extended the power available to provisional liquidators in order to deal adequately with dishonesty or malpractice on the part of bankrupts or company directors.

It was settled law that in neither a public nor a private examination could a bankrupt invoke the privilege against self-incrimination and refuse to answer questions. It would therefore be illogical if a company director could maintain silence on a private examination under section 235 or 236.

In practically every case where a provisional liquidator wanted to question a director, there would have been a failure to keep proper accounting records, and a potential liability for false accounting under the Theft Act 1968. There would be no point in such an examination if the director was entitled to keep silent on the ground of possible self-incrimination.

Again, *in Re Arrows Ltd*, the Chancery Division of the High Court stated that a former managing director was not entitled to refuse to answer questions or to supply documents when an order had been made under section 236 of the Act of 1986, even after he had been charged with criminal offences in relation to the company. Mr Justice Vinelott ruled that on the facts of the case the importance to the liquidators of completing their enquiries outweighed any oppression to the director. He was not entitled to refuse to answer questions on the ground of possible self-incrimination.

In relation to the powers of DTI Inspectors to insist on their questions being answered, the case of *Re London United Investments plc* has given guidance.

The case concerned the circumstances surrounding payments of commission on reinsurance contracts. DTI inspectors wished to interview a director. Civil proceedings for fraud had been commenced against the director in respect of the alleged diversion of commission. It was argued on behalf of the director that it was improper for inspectors to investigate matters involving fraud, because it was more appropriate that suspected crimes should be investigated by the Serious Fraud Office or by the police. The Court of Appeal decided that this argument was wrong, and that the common law privilege against self-incrimination did not apply.

4 Liabilities

Statutory Liabilities: Minimum Membership

Where a company carries on business with less than two members, for a period of more than six months, then a member of the company who knows of these facts is personally liable for the debts of the company contracted during that period. The company may also be wound up by the court. Although this rule does not expressly apply to directors, it will of course affect directors who are also members of the company.

Prospectus

A prospectus is defined as "any prospectus, notice, circular, advertisement or other invitation, offering to the public for subscription or purchase any shares or debentures of a company". Where a prospectus contains false information, the following consequences may ensue.

- Under the general law of contract, purchasers may rescind their agreements.
- There may be a right to damages against directors responsible for issuing the prospectus.
- A right to an action in tort, for deceit, may arise. This will again result in an award of damages.
- Damages may also be available for the tort of negligent misrepresentation.
- Criminal liability under the Theft Act 1968. (See Chapter 7.)

Allotment of Shares

The allotment of shares by directors must be carried out on the best terms obtainable. Shares must not be allotted to themselves or their friends at a lower price in order to obtain

Figure 3: Liability for Prospectus – Five Potential Consequences

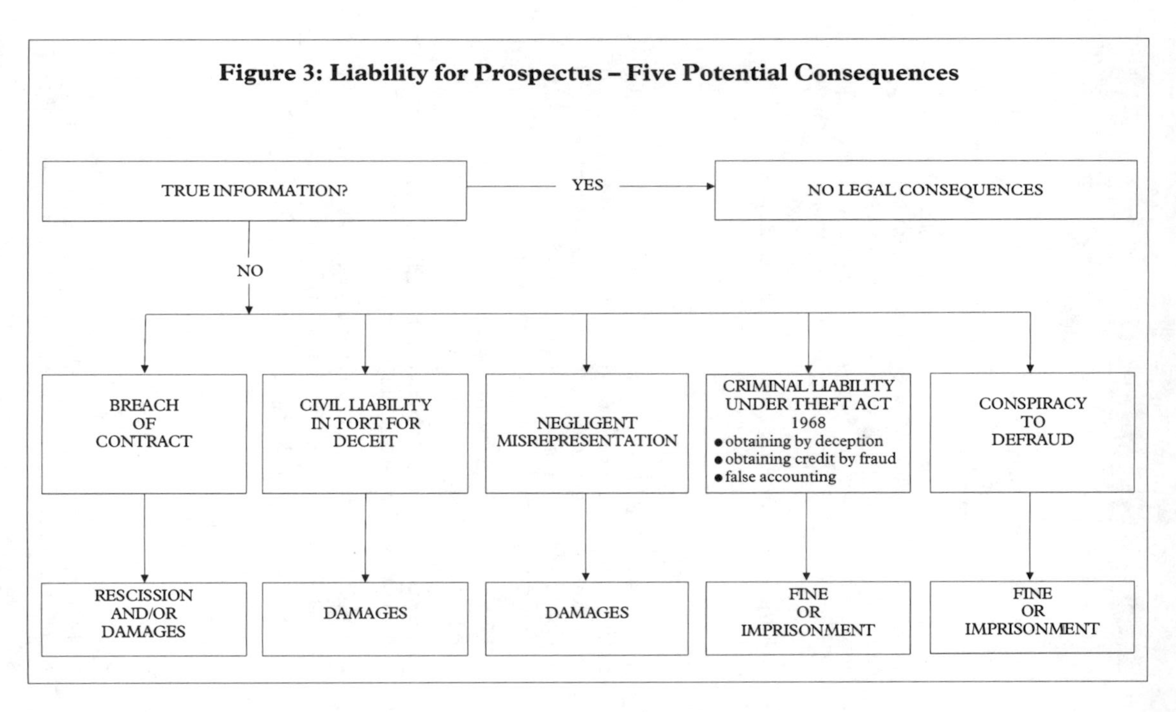

a personal benefit. Directors must act bona fide for the interests of the company. Any profit which is made from the improper allotment of shares will belong to the company.

The question of the allotment of shares from an improper motive is illustrated by *Bamford v Bamford* (1969). The Articles of the company provided that all unissued shares were to be at the disposal of the directors. The directors allotted shares to a particular person in order to prevent a takeover bid. Fraud was not at issue. The members by resolution in general meeting later ratified the issue. The Court of Appeal held that where directors act *intra vires* the company but *ultra vires* their own powers in that they issue shares with an improper motive, such act may be validated by the members of the company in general meeting, provided that a full and frank disclosure is made to them.

Misfeasance

Misfeasance arises when directors have misapplied, retained or become accountable for company property or money. In such circumstances, a liquidator may apply to the court for an order for repayment of the money, restoration of the property, or a contribution to the lost assets. Dishonesty need not be proved.

A recent example is *Re Purpont* (1991). In that case a director, knowing that the company was unable to pay its trade debts as they fell due, bought a car on behalf of the company but which was not needed for the company's purposes and withdrew cash from the company's account. The High Court ruled that he should repay the cost of the car, and the cash, to the liquidator. The director should have realised that the company could not avoid insolvent liquidation.

Wrongful Trading

Section 214 of the Insolvency Act 1986 obliges directors to analyse the financial state of their company. If they conclude that there is no reasonable prospect of avoiding insolvent liquidation, they have a duty to take every step which a reasonably diligent person would take to minimise potential loss to the company's creditors. If a director fails to comply with this duty then he may be ordered to make a contribution to the company's assets. The amount of such contribution is the amount by which the company's assets have been depleted. The liability of the director in these circumstances is assessed according to what a reasonable person should have known, not what the director himself knew.

Directors must therefore assess the reasonableness of avoiding insolvent liquidation. If they are unsure of the position, then they risk liability for wrongful trading. In reality, this means that if liquidation is a reasonable possibility they should protect their position by transferring control to an insolvency practitioner. The director is not obliged to cease trading when a problem is identified but must obtain full information about the prospects and keep the possibility of insolvent liquidation under review. If the director proceeds on the basis of proper professional advice then wrongful trading liability should be avoided.

Fraudulent Preference

A company director instructed Company X to transfer money to Company Y. Both companies were insolvent. The effect of the transaction was to reduce the director's liability under a personal guarantee of Company Y's debts. The Court of Appeal stated that this was both a fraudulent preference and a misfeasance and that the money should be repaid by the director to the liquidator, with interest (*Liquidator of West Mercia Safetywear v Dodd* (1988)).

Insolvency

When a company gets into financial difficulties, directors have a number of legal duties. Possible liabilities may arise in respect of wrongful trading, fraudulent trading, general fiduciary duties and disqualification.

Where it appears that the assets of a company may not cover its debts and that a potential insolvency situation has arisen, then independent professional advice should be sought. The Insolvency Act 1986 has provided a number of procedures which may help the company to survive. These are:

- arrangements with creditors
- reconstruction or amalgamation
- administration orders
- receivership
- voluntary winding up
- compulsory winding up.

The appointment of an administrator may amount to an act which minimises potential losses to creditors and thus may avoid liability for wrongful trading. The Court must be petitioned for such an appointment. It will make an administration order in a number of circumstances including the likelihood of the company's survival, compromise with creditors or a more advantageous realisation of the company's assets than if it was subjected to winding up.

The administrator prepares a formal statement of proposals which is put to a creditors' meeting. If the statement is approved, the administrator is given very wide powers to run the company. He may appoint or dismiss directors.

Receivership

Where a company is unable to pay money secured by a debenture, the debenture holder may appoint a receiver to take control of the company's financial affairs. The powers of a receiver are very similar to those of an administrator.

Voluntary Winding Up

This is effected by a shareholders' resolution that the company be wound up. It may be a members' voluntary winding up where the directors state that the company will be able to pay its debts in full in a period not more than 12 months from the commencement of the winding up. A director who makes such a statement unreasonably is guilty of a criminal offence.

A liquidator will normally be appointed in a voluntary winding up. His appointment terminates the powers of the directors. The role of the liquidator is to realise the assets of the company and to pay its debts.

Compulsory Winding Up

This is effected by the court. The following persons may apply:

- the company itself
- directors
- the Secretary of State for Trade and Industry
- shareholders
- creditors
- the official receiver
- an administrator or administrative receiver.

Where the court accepts the application, it will appoint the official receiver as provisional liquidator. Directors have a duty to supply information to the provisional liquidator. When the liquidator has realised all the assets and paid off the debts as far as possible, the company will be dissolved after the completion of a number of formalities.

Contempt

The application of the law of contempt to directors was discussed in the case of *Re Agreements Relating To Supply of Ready-mixed Concrete* (1989). A court order had been made prohibiting two companies from giving effect to restrictive trade practices. The Director-General of Fair Trading sought orders committing directors of companies to prison for contempt. It was accepted that the directors had not been involved in the contempts. It was held in the High Court that directors could not be liable for contempt solely by virtue of their office, there must be knowledge or involvement in the commission of the contempt.

Theft

See Chapter 7.

Bribery

In *Hannibal & Co v Frost* (1988) a company sued its former

managing director for money withdrawn by him from the company. He pleaded that the money had been paid to a third party as a bribe on behalf of the company and that, in consequence, the company had benefited by having substantial contracts awarded to it. The Court of Appeal ruled that the managing director had no defence. A director has no power or authority to give a bribe on the company's behalf. The money withdrawn from the company had been stolen and the company was entitled to its return.

Ultra Vires

This is an old-established rule of company law which states that acts outside the scope of the company's objects (as stated in the memorandum of association) are void. Although the rule is of less significance than formerly, mainly because objects clauses can be so widely drafted as to include almost any commercial act, directors must still be aware of it. They should, in particular, be aware of the scope of the objects clause and ensure that the company keeps within its scope. Otherwise they may incur personal liability for *ultra vires* acts.

An example of the application of the rule is *Viscount of the Royal Court of Jersey v Shelton* (1986). A Jersey company agreed to buy property in England. After some payments had been made, the company became insolvent. The Viscount took proceedings in the Jersey court against the directors of the company for their loss on the basis that the agreement had been *ultra vires* the objects of the company. There was no allegation of dishonesty.

Under the company's articles of association, the directors were entitled to be indemnified against all losses incurred in the conduct of the company's business, and no director was to be liable for any loss which should happen in the course of the duties of his office unless the same should happen through his own dishonesty.

The Privy Council ruled that the effect of these provisions was to exonerate directors from personal liability. In the absence of dishonesty the directors were not liable for *ultra vires* acts.

Remedies

Statutory Remedies

Section 212 of the Insolvency Act 1986 states that, in a winding up, directors may be examined by the court as to their conduct, and may be ordered to repay, restore or account for the company's assets. The section does not create new rights. It confers a discretion upon the court as to whether an order is made, and as to the amount of relief given.

Section 727 of the Companies Act 1985 provides that in any proceedings against a director for negligence, default, breach of duty or breach of trust, if a director has in the opinion of the court acted honestly and reasonably and ought fairly to be excused, then he may be wholly or partly relieved. The section has given rise to a number of procedural problems, examples of which follow.

In *Re Kirby's Coaches* (1991), on a misfeasance summons, the directors of R pleaded in their defence that they had acted honestly and reasonably and ought to be excused from liability. The decision in the case was that the burden of proof was upon the directors but that they need not raise the issue until trial.

In *Re Duomatic* (1969) it was stated that a director is regarded as having acted reasonably if he has acted in the way in which a man of affairs with reasonable care and circumspection could reasonably be expected to act in such a case.

In *Re Gilt Edge Safety Glass Ltd* (1940) directors were prosecuted for having acted without the necessary qualification shares. The magistrates adjourned the matter to enable the defendants to seek relief under the provision which preceded section 727. It was held that the only court which can give relief is the court before which proceedings are brought.

Common Law Remedies

- Summary termination of a director's service contract by

dismissal in a case of gross misconduct. Serious misconduct meriting instant dismissal could take many forms, including:

- violence or fighting at work
- foul language and intimidating or antisocial behaviour
- dishonesty
- indecent behaviour
- obviously criminal acts.

- An order for a director to restore company property which is in his possession.
- An injunction or declaration to prevent directors acting outside the scope of their powers.
- Damages. The amount of damages payable will be either the loss suffered by the company or the profit gained by the director. A director against whom damages are awarded may recover contribution from any other person liable in respect of the same damage.
- Rescission of contracts with the company. The aim of the court in such cases is to achieve practical justice between the parties.
- An account of profits. In the case of a secret profit the court may allow a director an allowance for reasonable remuneration for work carried out in effecting the transaction.

Product Liability

The Consumer Protection Act 1987 imposed strict liability upon producers where a defective product causes personal injury or damage to the property of a consumer.

"Producer" for these purposes includes the manufacturer, an importer of goods into the EEC and in some circumstances the supplier.

"Product" means any goods or electricity and includes products which are comprised in other products. The word "goods" is further defined as including "substances, growing crops and things comprised in land by virtue of being attached to it and any ship, aircraft or vehicle".

These definitions can cause problems, particularly in relation to intellectual property such as books and computer software.

The scope of the word "defective" is also far from clear. Section 3(1) of the Act states that a product is defective where its "safety" is not such as persons generally are entitled to expect. Section 3(2) sets out a number of features of "safety" which the courts may take into account, including:

- The manner in which, and the purposes for which, the product has been marketed, and instructions and warnings supplied with the product
- Reasonable expectations as to what might be done with the product.
- The time at which the product was supplied.

The scope of the Act of 1987 is limited by a number of specific defences. The most important and controversial of these is the so-called "development risks" defence which provides that a producer may not be liable if it can be shown that the state of scientific and technical knowledge at the relevant time was not such that a producer of products of the same description as the product in question might be expected to have discovered the defect if it had existed in his products while they were under his control.

Further, the plaintiff must prove that the damage was actually caused wholly or partly by the defect in the product. There is no requirement of foreseeability on the part of the producer.

"Damage", for the purpose of the Act, is limited to situations where the property was intended for private use. Damage to business property is excluded.

The Act has been criticised because it has led to higher insurance premiums which have been passed on to the consumer.

See Appendix.

Vicarious Liability

The effect of the principle of vicarious liability is that an employer may be liable for civil wrongs committed by an employee. Directors should be aware that in certain circumstances the behaviour of their employees in the course of their work may make the employer liable for damages. Further, where a director is himself an employee, and commits civil wrongs, this may make the company itself vicariously liable.

A classic example of the practical implications of this doctrine is the case of *Century Insurance Co. v Northern Ireland Road Transport Board* (1942). A petrol tanker driver lit a cigarette while delivering petrol to a garage. He threw away the lighted match and caused an explosion. His employer was held liable for the damage caused by the explosion on the basis that at the time of the accident the driver was doing what he was employed to do, even though it had been done in a negligent way.

The reasoning behind the application of such a rule is, generally, that an employer is better able to compensate victims of accidents caused by employees than the employee himself. An employee will often not be worth suing. The requirements for the application of the principle are as follows:

- There must be a genuine relationship of employer and employee.
- The employee must have committed a civil wrong.
- The wrong must have been committed in the course of the employment. This has caused considerable difficulty, because no one is ever actually employed with the aim of incurring civil liability. The following cases illustrate the complexity of the problem.

Conway v George Wimpey & Co. Ltd (1951). The employers provided transport for their emplyees on a building site. The drivers were expressly prohibited from giving lifts to employees of other companies. One driver broke this rule, and as a result of his negligence an employee of another company was injured. The Court of Appeal ruled that there was no vicarious liability because at the time of the accident the driver was doing an unauthorised and prohibited act.

Williams v Hemphill Ltd (1966). A driver had departed from his authorised route when giving some boys a lift home. During the detour the boys were injured in an accident. A Scottish court ruled that the driver's employers were liable: the accident had occured in the course of the driver's employment.

Heasmans v Clarity Cleaning Co. (1987). The defendants employed people to clean offices. One of them used a client's telephone to make unauthorised international calls worth more than £1000. The court ruled that the employers were not vicariously liable: the employee had done a totally unauthorised act, outside the scope of the emplyment.

Irving v The Post Office (1987). A postman had quarrelled with his neighbours who were of Jamaican origin. During the course of sorting mail, he wrote on the back of a letter addressed to the neighbours "Go home Sambo" and drew a black smiling face. The neighbours claimed that the Post Office were vicariously liable for this act of racial abuse by an employee. The Court of Appeal stated that the act was one of "personal malevolence" and could not be said to have been within the course of employment. It is clear that, where an employer has been found vicariously liable, he may claim back from the employee any amount which he has been ordered to pay in damages. This right of indemnity may, of course, be of largely theoretical value where the employee is of limited means.

5 Termination of Directorships

A director may cease to hold office in the following circumstances.

Resignation

The rules on resignation are to be found in the Articles. Table A states that notice of resignation must be given to the company without specifying any period. Form 288 must be completed and lodged. (See Chapter 2.)

In situations of threatened or potential insolvency, directors should be very cautious about retiring. The possibility of liability for wrongful or fraudulent trading with respect to transactions entered into before retirement should not be discounted.

End of Specified Period of Employment

Where a director is appointed for a specified period of time, he will automatically cease to hold office at the end of that period.

Removal

Section 303, Companies Act 1985, enables the company to remove a director by passing an ordinary resolution. An example of this is *Bushell v Faith* (1970) where the meaning of the words "ordinary resolution" were considered. The facts were that the 300 issued shares of a company were owned equally by A, B and C. The Articles provided that on a poll on a resolution for the removal of a director, any shares held by that director should have three votes per share. A and B proposed an ordinary resolution to remove C from his directorship. They voted for such removal and claimed that this resolution was passed by 200 votes to 100. C maintained that, by virtue of the provision in the Articles, the resolution had been defeated by 300 votes to 200, his own votes having three votes per share.

The House of Lords decided that the provision in the Articles was valid and that C's contention was correct. The words "ordinary resolution" merely connote a resolution depending for its passing on a simple majority of votes cast in conformity with the Articles. They do not connote a resolution passed by a majority of members. The Articles may validly attach additional votes to certain shares on certain occasions.

Where there are irregularities in the removal of a director from office, which are curable by going through the proper procedures, then the court will not intervene by way of interlocutory injunction.

This was the decision in *Bentley-Stevens v Jones* (1974) where A, B and C were directors of X Co. and of Y Co., a wholly-owned subsidiary. After a dispute, B and C held a board meeting. Notice of the meeting was sent to A but he did not receive it. At the meeting, B passed a resolution removing A from the board, without going through the correct procedures. A sought an injunction to prevent B and C carrying out the terms of the resolution. This was refused. The irregularities could be cured by going through the proper process.

Again, in *Bersel Manufacturing Co v Berry* (1968), H and W were the incorporators of a private company. The Articles provided that they should be permanent life directors and also stated that "the permanent life directors shall have power to terminate forthwith the directorship of any of the ordinary directors by notice in writing". H and W held between themselves the majority of issues shares in the company.

W died, and on her death B and her supporters obtained a majority of the shareholding. B was appointed an ordinary director, but H purported to terminate her directorship. B argued that this power had been given to H and W jointly and could not be exercised by the survivor.

The House of Lords ruled that the power of termination

was vested in H and W neither as a personal confidence nor as in persons holding an office such as executor or trustee. Upon its true construction, the power of termination survived the death of one of the donees and was capable of being exercised by the survivor.

In *Lee v Chou Wen Hsien* (1984) (a Hong Kong case) the Articles required a director to vacate his office if he was required to resign by all his co-directors. He was bound to do so even if the co-directors had acted for ulterior reasons. In the case itself, he was required to vacate office because he was concerned about the company's dealings and had requested the convening of a board meeting. His expulsion from the board was nevertheless effective.

Wrongfully dismissed directors may be able to claim compensation for wrongful dismissal, unfair dismissal or redundancy - this depends on general employment law. (See Chapter 6.)

Disqualification

This area of law has seen massive development in recent years. The Company Directors Disqualification Act 1986 states, in outline, that a person may not act as a director without the leave of the court in the following cases:

- undischarged bankruptcy
- failure to pay under a county court administration order
- where a director is subject to a disqualification order.

In *R v Campbell* a disqualification order was held to prevent a person from acting as a management consultant where this post involved the central management of the company.

Disqualification Orders

A court may make a disqualification order in the following circumstances:

- conviction of an indictable offence in connection with the promotion, formation, management or liquidation of a company or with the receivership or management of a company's property

- persistent breaches of the legislation in relation to returns, accounts or other documents
- fraud
- summary conviction for breaches of the legislation
- conduct appearing to the Secretary of State to make a person unfit to be concerned in the management of a company. The courts have stated that "unfitness" covers a very wide range of behaviour including gross incompetence involving a danger to the public with some element of "commercial immorality"
- participation in fraudulent or wrongful trading (See Chapter 3).

Recent examples of the way in which the courts have exercised their discretionary powers in this area are as follows.

Purpose Of Disqualification

Re Lo-Line Electric (1988): The purpose of disqualification is protection of the public rather than punishment of the director. The application of natural justice is crucial. Ordinary commercial mismanagement is not enough. A further point in the *Lo-Line* case was that the person against whom a disqualification order was sought had been a *de facto* rather than a *de jure* director: the Court of Appeal stated that the definition of the word "director" was wide enough to include a *de facto* director.

The most notorious of the recent decisions is that of Peter Clowes. He was disqualified from being a company director for the maximum period of 15 years after being convicted of eight charges of fraud and 10 of theft, totalling more than £14 million. The judge described the scale of the crimes as "breathtaking". He had diverted millions of pounds from investors on the fraudulent basis that their money would be invested in gilt-edged stock. In reality, he had spent the money on a luxury lifestyle including an executive jet, a yacht and a chateau in France.

Another example is the recent case of *Re Melcast*, where X and Y, who were directors, had continued to run a company despite knowing that it was in severe financial difficulty and having received warnings from an insolvency practitioner. The company ceased trading in 1987, with debts of £1 million. Applications were made to disqualify the two from being directors or taking part in the promotion, formation or management of a company. X was disqualified for four years and Y for seven. X did not have as much knowledge of the position of the company as Y and had little idea of the scope of his duties as a director. Y had shown gross irresponsibility. He was aged 68, and because of this a seven-year period was appropriate to protect the public. If he had been younger he would have been disqualified for 10 years.

In *Re Tansoft*, another recent case, the official receiver applied to disqualify A who had been the director of three associated companies dealing in computer products. The companies were liquidated, leaving liabilities of £130,000, £6 million and £108,000. It was alleged that A had not made annual returns and had failed to co-operate with the official receiver. It was also stated that money belonging to one company had been misappropriated to buy a flat in Spain and that the assets of another company had been sold to another in which A had an interest, and where the selling company was unlikely to receive payment for its assets.

A was disqualified for seven years. His behaviour made him unfit to be a director. It was a bad case of repeated failure to attain the standards of those responsible for the management of companies.

On the other hand, in *Re ECM Electronics*, an application was made to disqualify a managing director on the grounds that he had failed to file accounts for one year, had paid excessive remuneration, failed to co-operate with the receivers, attempted to misuse the company name, made unjustified payments to his wife, held meetings without notice and made himself a prohibited loan. The application was dismissed on the basis that there had been no gross negligence or incompetence. There had been a falling from standards which ought to have been maintained but this did not amount to a breach of commercial morality and there was no "unfitness".

Recent guidance has been given by the Court of Appeal on periods of disqualification to be imposed:

- 10 years plus – particularly serious cases, for example a second disqualification.
- Middle range 6 to 10 years – serious cases.
- Lower end of scale: 2 to 5 years – not very serious cases. For example a director who was not dishonest, but extremely incompetent, should be disqualified for five years.

The Court of Appeal has also recently ruled on the meaning of section 2 of the Act of 1986, which states that an application for a disqualification order should not be made more than two years after a company becomes insolvent, except with the leave of the court. In *Official Receiver v Nixon*, the Appeal Court stated that leave will be given to apply out of time if there is an arguable case for disqualification, an adequate explanation for the delay, and no prejudice to the person against whom the disqualification order is sought.

Again, in *Re Majestic Recording Studios*, the official receiver applied for disqualification orders in respect of a director of companies which had failed to submit accounts and annual returns. The director argued that the order should not be made because he had no control over financial matters and did not know why the accounts had not been filed. This argument was rejected. The public was entitled to protection against a person who had failed to fulfil the duties connected with the privilege of limited liability.

Disobedience of a disqualification order results in criminal liability on the part of both the company and the individual director.

In *Re Swift* (1992), X was director of a number of groups of companies. The first group consisted of six separate companies which had traded in succession to each other, each following on the insolvency of its predecessor. X did not control the day-to-day running of the companies.

The second group of companies had failed to file returns and accounts. Inter-group transactions had not been properly recorded, with the result that when the companies became insolvent it was impossible for the liquidator to trace assets and debts attributable to the companies.

In respect of two other groups of companies, X was alleged to have failed to comply with the Companies Act 1985.

X was disqualified from being a company director for three years. Mr Justice Hoffman stated that his directorship of the first group of companies had demonstrated a "lack of commercial morality" which the Act of 1986 had sought to prohibit. Although X had not been directly concerned in the day-to-day running of the companies, he was not absolved of responsibility. The running of the companies demonstrated unfitness to act as a director, although this was not particularly serious. The fact that X had personally guaranteed the liabilities of the companies, and as a result had become bankrupt and had lost his house, was also taken into account.

Disqualification of Directors Following Health and Safety Convictions

It is now clear that section 2 of the Company Directors Disqualification Act 1986 applies to health and safety matters. The Act provides for courts to make disqualification orders against persons convicted of indictable offences connected with the promotion, formation, management or liquidation of a company. "Management" includes the management of health and safety.

The first case to be decided on these grounds was that of Rodney Chapman, a director of Chapman Chalk Supplies Ltd. The company had been served a prohibition notice on the basis that it had carried out quarrying work in an unsafe manner resulting in significant danger from rock falls. Both the company and Mr Chapman were prosecuted for contravening the terms of the prohibition notice. Each was fined £5000. It was stated that Mr Chapman had known the dangers in the quarry but had still placed men in great danger and had deliberatly continued to extract minerals without a safe system of work. Mr Chapman was disqualified from being a company director for two years.

Summary: Disqualification – Matters Which a Court Will Take into Account

When company is solvent or insolvent

- Breach of duty by director
- Misapplication of company property
- Responsibility for transactions defrauding creditors
- Failure to comply with rules as to company accounts

When company is insolvent

- Responsibility for causes of insolvency
- Failure to supply goods or services which have been paid for
- Entering into transactions liable to be set aside
- Responsibility for failure to call creditors' meeting
- Failure to co-operate with liquidator

6 Responsibility for Employees

Directors as Employers and/or Employees

A director may be both an employee, in the terms of his service contract with the company, and an employer. The general law of employment, which is developing with great speed and complexity, will apply to both capacities. Directors who do not comply with employment law may find themselves subject to a variety of consequences including appearing as witnesses in an industrial tribunal, or being on the receiving end of a writ in civil proceedings, or being prosecuted for breaches of the health and safety legislation.

Meaning of Employment

There is no clear legal definition of employment. The courts have adopted a so-called "multiple" test which involves considering the questions set out below.

Checklist: Employed v Self-employed

- Have the parties described themselves as employer and employee in the contract?
- Is the person working *integrated* in the business – for example, does the employer give sickness and holiday entitlement?
- Who controls the manner, time and place of work?
- Who provides the tools, equipment and premises?
- Who takes the financial risk?
- Who takes the chance of profit?
- Who pays PAYE and national insurance contributions?
- Is the person working *on their own account*?

The employment status of a director was raised in the case of *Parsons v Parsons* (1979). P was a director, with his brothers, of a family business. After disagreements it was resolved, at an extraordinary general meeting, to remove him from office. He claimed compensation for unfair dismissal. The Court of Appeal ruled that he was not an employee. He had not been treated as such in the company's documents. Despite the fact that he was an executive director who worked at the business every day, he had received no salary as such, paid national insurance contributions as a self-employed person and had no contract of employment.

The general rule is that working directors are normally employees for the purposes of employment legislation. This case shows that, given the right combination of facts, courts will go against the conventional view. The key factor in the case was the way the directors were treated in the company's accounts.

Controlling Directorships

In *Road Transport Industry Training Board v Readers Garage* (1969) the managing director of a company owned 99½% of the shares. An industrial tribunal found that he could not be regarded as an employee because of his controlling position. The High Court stated that his controlling position did not necessarily preclude him from being an employee, and that there could be an implied contract of service.

Responsibilities as Employers

Recruitment of Employees

It is unlawful to discriminate on the grounds of sex or race in the recruitment of staff. In particular, this means that advertisements must not be written in a way that may be considered discriminatory, for example by the use of "he" throughout, or expressions such as "Girl Friday". At interviews, applicants are entitled to be given a similar format for the interview. They are entitled to be asked broadly the same questions as their competitors.

It may be discrimination for female applicants to be asked

questions such as "When are you going to get married?" or "When are you going to have children?" Male applicants are not normally asked these questions.

Applicants belonging to an ethnic minority are entitled not to be asked questions about their racial or ethnic background which would not be asked of white applicants.

The Disabled Persons (Employment) Acts 1944 and 1958 state that employers with more than 20 regular workers must employ a quota of registered disabled workers.

Contracts of Employment

Within 13 weeks of the start of employment, an employer must provide the employee with written particulars of the terms of employment. This must contain the following details:

- name of employer and employee
- date of commencement of employment
- job title
- hours worked
- terms of holidays and holiday pay
- details of notice of termination
- disciplinary and grievance procedures
- sickness or injury provisions
- pension arrangements.
- if the employment is for a fixed term, the date of expiry.

A leading case on the interpretation of a director's contract of employment is *Thomas Marshall (Exporters) Ltd v Guinle* (1978).

The facts were that G was appointed managing director of a company for a fixed term of 10 years. A major part of his work involved travel abroad arranging contracts. The success of the company depended heavily upon G's business contacts abroad. His contract contained restrictions, for example prohibiting the disclosure of confidential information; banning work in any other business; and restricting his employment of company employees for five years after the end of his contract of employment.

It was discovered that G had set up his own company in the same line of business, had purchased goods for it abroad while on company business, had solicited customers and had employed four ex-employees. When G was invited to discuss matters he resigned his post. The company sought an injunction to prevent further breaches of the contract. G argued that his own breaches of the contract had effectively brought it to an end and that he was therefore free from the restrictions in it.

The High Court gave the injunction asked for. It was up to the employers to elect what their course of action would be, whether to accept G's resignation or to refuse it and to hold him to the terms of the agreement. G's contract did not automatically end because of his repudiation of it.

Deductions From Wages

Unauthorised deductions from the wages of an employee may result in a claim to an industrial tribunal under the Wages Act. Deductions may lawfully be made in the following circumstances:

- attachment orders
- PAYE income tax
- national insurance contributions
- deductions expressly permitted under the contract of employment
- written consent by the employee
- retail trades: in very limited circumstances, deductions may be made to meet cash shortages or stock deficiencies.

The case of *Delaney v Staples* (House of Lords 1992) illustrates the current law on deductions from wages, as well as questions of the jurisdiction of industrial tribunals and procedures in the industrial tribunal system. The case involved a claim for less than £150, but it nevertheless went through the whole of the legal system, from industrial tribunal to Employment Appeal Tribunal, then to the Court of Appeal and the House of Lords. The key point in the case was that payments in lieu of notice are not "wages" and must be recovered in the county court and not the industrial tribunal.

Health And Safety At Work

The rights of both employers and employees to health and safety at work are protected in two main ways.

- By the general common law of negligence, which imposes upon employers the duty to provide a safe system of working. This means ensuring a safe working environment and providing information, training and supervision.
- By specific legislation, including the Factories Act 1961 and the Health and Safety at Work etc Act 1974.

The consequences of inattention to health and safety measures are severe, possibly resulting in serious injury, illness or even death.

The areas of law most relevant to health and safety at work are:

- The Health and Safety at Work Act with its attendant Regulations and Approved Codes of Practice
- The Factories Act 1961 and consequent Regulations
- The Offices, Shops and Railway Premises Act 1963 and consequent Regulations
- Case law developed to interpret the above legislation
- The tort of negligence
- Employment law and the civil law duties based upon it.
- Directors must also be aware of EC directives relating to health and safety and their impact on domestic legislation. (See page 86.) *See also Croner's Reference Book for Employers.*

Civil Liabilities

Safety of Premises

This civil duty originates from the Occupiers' Liability Acts 1957 and 1984. The occupiers of property are liable for risks to persons on the premises resulting from dangerous conditions (for example unsafe stairways or blocked passages).

Safety of Manufactured Goods

Manufacturers must take reasonable care to ensure that their products are without defect and not liable to cause injury. But where a purchaser observes a defect and nevertheless continues to use it, the manufacturer is no longer liable.

Employers' Liability

Employers are responsible for their employees' safety during working hours. The common law duty of care, which is now also a statutory duty under section 2 of the Health and Safety at Work Act, covers the following broad areas.

- Provision of a safe system of work including choice of working methods and process layout.
- Maintenance of the workplace in a safe condition
- Provision of safe and suitable plant and equipment, which must be adequately maintained. This includes personal protective equipment. The provisions of the Factories Act 1961 set out criteria for safety, including the guarding or fencing of dangerous machinery.
- Supervision and instruction of employees, especially those who are young and inexperienced.
- Selection of employees, for example the dismissal of those known to be troublemakers of whose behaviour jeopardises the safety of others. Any question of dismissal must be carefully dealt with in accordance with the general requirements of employment law.

Defences

If an employer/director is sued for negligence, a number of potential defences are available:

- denial of liability
- contributory negligence, that is, the plaintiff was partly responsible for the accident and damages should be reduced accordingly
- a third party was wholly or partly responsible for the accident
- knowing acceptance of the risk by the employee. This defence, known technically as *volenti*, has virtually ceased to exist
- limitation. Actions for damages for personal injuries must, as a rule, be brought within three years from the date of the accident. This is subject to a number of exceptions. Specifically, in certain cases of disease, the three-year period begins only when the victim becomes aware of the symptoms.

The Health and Safety at Work etc Act 1974

The Health and Safety at Work etc Act 1974 was a revolutionary piece of legislation. It applies to all forms of work activity and covers anyone at risk from accident or disease, whether or not they are employed at particular premises. Employees and the self-employed, as well as employers, are held responsible for the health and safety of themselves and others.

The Act is also an enabling statute, that is it gives the responsible minister power to make Regulations which apply to specific situations and give detailed practical instructions. A major example of this is the Control of Substances Hazardous to Health Regulations (COSHH).

Enforcement

The 1974 Act set up the Health and Safety Executive which is responsible for its enforcement, carried out by inspectors. Inspectors have the following powers:

- entry and inspection of premises
- taking measurements and samples
- obtaining information
- seizure and destruction of articles or substances causing imminent danger or risk of serious personal injury

- issue of prohibition notice. This requires cessation of hazardous activity where such activity involves the likely risk of serious personal injury
- issue of improvement notice. This states a time limit within which dangerous practices must be remedied.

Case Law

The very general definition of duties under the 1974 Act creates the same kind of problems of interpretation as those which arise in civil negligence cases and in company law. Obligations are qualified by phrases such as "reasonably practicable". In general terms, the courts have ruled that this phrase means balancing the degree of risk against the cost and inconvenience of overcoming it.

Management of Health and Safety at Work Regulations 1992

These Regulations came into force on 1 January 1993. They incorporate into English law the requirements of EEC Directive 89/391. The Directive essentially restates existing English health and safety law in great detail and does not make many changes, but there are two important additions:

- Employers will be expressly required to make risk assessments.
- Proper management processes must be set up for the conduct of health and safety at work.

Again, it is important to note that directors may find themselves in the position of both employer and employee for the purposes of these Regulations, where they have a contract of employment with their company. Self-employed directors with no employees must also take cognisance of the new rules.

In relation to risk assessment, the new requirement is that employers must carefully assess risks to the health and safety of employees and others who might be exposed to risk in their undertakings, for example visitors and customers. The self-employed have similar obligations.

Particular attention must be paid to the state of vehicles used for company business and to persons working alone. The assessment must be made in writing where there are five or more employees.

Summary: Health and Safety at Work Rules

Statutes

- Factories Act 1961
- Offices, Shops and Railway Premises Act 1963
- Employer's Liability (Defective Equipment) Act 1969
- Fire Precautions Act 1971
- Health and Safety at Work Act 1974
- Occupiers' Liability Act 1984

Examples of regulations

- Construction (Working Places) Regulations 1966
- Protection of Eyes Regulations 1974
- Asbestos Regulations
- Notification of Accidents and Dangerous Occurences Regulations
- Control of Substances Hazardous to Health Regulations

Breaches of these rules may lead to both civil claims for compensation and criminal liability. Cases involving criminal prosecution of directors for health and safety offences are dealt with in Chapter 7.

Trade Union Membership

In relation to the trade union rights of employees, the responsibilities of employers include:

- communicating information on collective bargaining
- consultation on possible redundancies

- consultation in respect of a planned transfer of an undertaking
- appointment of safety representatives.

Employees also have rights to time off work for union training and activities.

Termination of Employment

Wrongful Dismissal

This occurs where an employee is dismissed with less notice than he is entitled to receive under his contract of employment, or is dismissed before the expiry of a fixed-term contract. In other words it involves breach of contract and therefore is dealt with in the county court and not the industrial tribunal. It is an independent and separate claim from *unfair dismissal.* A major recent example is *Dietman v London Borough of Brent* (1988) where D was a senior social worker who was summarily dismissed as a result of the Jasmine Beckford affair. The dismissal was for "gross misconduct" and she was given no opportunity to state her case. The Court of Appeal ruled that the dismissal had been wrongful and D was entitled to damages. Her behaviour had amounted to gross negligence, not gross misconduct, and in any event there should have been a formal disciplinary meeting.

Unfair Dismissal

The first legal protection against unfair dismissal was created in 1971. Before then, a dismissed employee's only remedy was to go to court to show breach of his or her employment contract by the employer. The right to sue for breach of his or her contract of employment still exists, but making a claim to a tribunal for unfair dismissal has largely replaced it in appropriate cases. Where dismissal is admitted by the employer, then the employer must show that the reason for the dismissal fell within one of the following categories:

- Misconduct.
- Poor capability or qualifications.
- Redundancy.

- Unlawfulness.
- Some other substantial reason.

The tribunal will then consider whether the dismissal was unfair, depending on whether in the circumstances the employer acted reasonably, and on the basis of equity and the substantial merits of the case.

Constructive Dismissal

Constructive or implied dismissal occurs where the employer's conduct is a serious breach of contract entitling the employee to leave without notice.

A significant decided case on dismissal of directors is *Norwest Holst Group Administration Ltd v Harrison* (1984). In that case H was a regional director in charge of the company's design office in Derby. In 1982 the regional managing director informed him that the design office was to be closed and went on to state that H would be based at a different office and that his new post would not carry a directorship. H objected to this and argued that it amounted to a dismissal on the grounds of redundancy. He also replied that he would be happy to accept 12 months' salary in lieu of notice and his statutory redundancy entitlement. His letter concluded as follows:

> *I would ask you to contact me immediately if you feel I have misunderstood what has been said or if further discussion would assist an amicable resolution of the matter.*

After some negotiation, the company offered to continue H's directorship. In the meantime, H left the company and took up another job. He then claimed compensation for unfair dismissal from the company.

The Employment Appeal Tribunal found that there had been no constructive dismissal and that therefore there was no ground for compensation for unfair dismissal. An employer is guilty of constructive dismissal when he commits some act which amounts to a serious breach of contract against the employee. The employee then has two choices: He may continue with the contract as before or he may opt to terminate the contract by resigning. Only if he chooses the latter course does the employer's action harden into a dismissal.

Another example is *Sheffield v Oxford Controls Co Ltd* (1979). In that case, S was a co-founder and equal shareholder of Oxford Controls. His relative share slipped to less than half when further capital was subscribed by a new shareholder. There had been tension between S and his co-founder, R. R offered S £10,000 to go. An agreement was drawn up which was preceded by a letter from R as follows:

> *If you do not resign I now feel it is in the Company's interests that I take steps to reconstitute the board. If we cannot agree upon the terms of your resignation I must give you notice of my intention to use my votes to remove you from the board.*

S signed the agreement but later claimed unfair dismissal. The decision of the tribunal was that there had been no dismissal. The willingness to resign had been brought about by a negotiation of satisfactory terms and not a "resign or be sacked" threat.

Again, in *Cox Toner v Crook* (1981) an employee director travelled abroad in 1979 without notifying his fellow directors. They complained about this and threatened to dismiss him for misconduct. Seven months later he told them that he would resign unless the allegations were withdrawn. They were not, and he resigned. He claimed that he had been constructively dismissed. The industrial tribunal found that the employers had repudiated the contract of employment and that the employee had been unfairly dismissed. The employers appealed.

The Employment Appeal Tribunal allowed the appeal on the ground that the fact that the employee had continued to work for seven months after the alleged repudiation meant that he had affirmed the contract.

Dismissal on Grounds of Risk to Health

The risk of ill-health is not a good reason for dismissal unless the risk is such that it creates a safety hazard.

In *Converfoam (Darwen) Ltd v Bell* (1981), B, a director, was absent from work for three months following a heart attack. He proposed to return to part-time work. Because of the risk of a recurrence he was asked to accept a lower paid job with less responsibility. He refused and was dismissed. The employers argued that the risk of another heart attack aggravated by B's tenure of directorship gave them a valid ground for dismissal. The tribunal decided that this argument was wrong. Only in exceptional circumstances could risk of illness be grounds for dismissal. The risk of illness would have to present a safety hazard to justify dismissal.

Redundancy

Redundancies arise when an employer's requirement for work of a particular kind done by an employee has ceased or diminished, temporarily or permanently. Redundancy situations have the following legal consequences:

- a duty to consult trade unions
- the duty to treat employees fairly
- special rules in relation to the transfer of ownership of a business
- redundancy payments.

Reorganisations

In *E R Sutton v Revlon Overseas Corporation Ltd* (1973) the result of a management reorganisation was that S, the chief accountant of Revlon, was dismissed. The company found that they no longer needed the services of a chief accountant. His work was split equally among three junior employees. S claimed compensation for unfair dismissal. By the time the case came to the tribunal, the issue was whether S had been dismissed for redundancy. The decision was that the dismissal had been by reason of redundancy. The company's need for work of the type done by S had diminished. Consequently he was redundant.

Redundancy Payments

In *Secretary of State for Employment v Crane* (1988) C had been a full-time employee, shareholder and managing director of a family company. Between 1971 and 3 April 1984, he received only such remuneration as the company could afford to pay him. In the 12 weeks up to 3 April 1984 he had been paid approximately £159 per week. After that date he had received no remuneration because the company could not afford it. An industrial tribunal found that he was entitled to a redundancy payment out of the redundancy fund.

In calculating his average weekly remuneration, the tribunal ignored the weeks after 3 April 1984 on the ground that "no remuneration was payable". The Secretary of State appealed on the basis that the tribunal had failed to distinguish between weeks where no remuneration was "payable" and weeks where none was actually paid.

The appeal was dismissed. The words "no remuneration was payable" covered situations where no remuneration was legally required to be paid. This included circumstances where an employee agreed to work for no pay, or where his contractual remuneration was effectively whatever sum the company could afford to pay — which could be nil, as in this case. The tribunal had been right to ignore the weeks after 3 April 1984.

7 Criminal Liability

The leading case on the liability of a company and its directors for general criminal offences outside the Companies Acts is *Tesco v Nattrass* (House of Lords, 1971). In that case Tesco had set up a careful and elaborate system of supervision of employees to ensure that offences against the Trade Descriptions Act 1968 were not committed. A store manager failed to check the conduct of his staff, and as a result a "Special Offer" poster was displayed when no such goods were in fact available.

The company was charged with an offence under the 1968 Act, and was eventually found not guilty. The case is most important because the House of Lords stated that a company may be criminally liable only for the acts of the board of directors, the managing director and perhaps other superior officers of the company who carry out the functions of management and who speak and act as the company.

The House of Lords referred to the "brains" of the company as "the person who is in actual control of the operations of the company or of a part of them and who is not responsible to another person in the company for the manner in which he discharges his duties in the sense of being under his orders".

Another significant decision is that of *R v Robert Millar Ltd* (1970) where a limited company and one of its directors were convicted of aiding and abetting causing death by dangerous driving. The director had instructed an employee to drive a lorry which he knew was in a defective and dangerous condition.

Health and Safety at Work

The following examples show recent decisions on the level of fines imposed upon directors for breaches of the Health and Safety at Work etc Act 1974. This Act aims to provide a code of general principles, to provide an enforcement procedure and to oversee compliance with the Act. It covers almost all employers, and it has been estimated that eight million people are protected by its provisions.

The Act states (section 2) that it shall be the duty of every employer to ensure, so far as is reasonably practicable, the health, safety and welfare at work of all his employees.

Section 37 provides for offences to be committed by individuals or corporate bodies, which include limited companies. In addition to prosecution of the corporate body, directors may be prosecuted individually if it is found that the offence was committed with the consent or connivance, or through the negligence of that person.

In 1991 the proprietor of the Leicester Waste Paper company was fined £1500 by Leicester magistrates for failing to ensure the health and safety of persons other than his employees during the transit of waste paper in a curtain-sided lorry. A bale of paper weighing 500kg had fallen on a person and injured him while the lorry was being unloaded. The load securing straps normally fitted to such vehicles had not been used.

In 1990 the managing director of Barratt East Midlands was fined £250 where his company had failed to maintain proper standards in relation to scaffolding on a building site. The managing director was convicted under section 37 on the basis that the company's offence was attributable to his neglect.

Corporate Manslaughter

Manslaughter has no clear meaning in English law. In general terms, it is a killing which falls short of murder because the killer had no intention to kill or to cause really serious physical harm to the victim.

In a number of European countries, companies can be liable for manslaughter. But it is more common for directors to be personally charged. For example, the president of the

French Football Federation was accused of manslaughter after the deaths of a number of supporters when a stand collapsed in a Corsica stadium.

A number of pressure groups are at present campaigning for changes in English prosecution practice in relation to corporate manslaughter. The problems have most recently been highlighted by the Marchioness case, where the husband of a victim of the Thames pleasure boat disaster brought a prosecution against the South Coast Shipping Company. The case was dismissed for evidential reasons, but the fact that the prosecutor was awarded costs may be seen as confirming that the prosecution of a company for manslaughter is valid under English law.

The principle that companies could be liable for manslaughter was first established in 1965. Gary Slapper, a senior lecturer at Staffordshire University, has pointed out that since that time 18,151 people have been killed at work without a single company having been convicted of homicide.

It cannot seriously be argued that the reason for this is that all the deaths have been "accidental", and not due to anyone's fault. The Health and Safety Executive's annual reports have repeatedly stated that the majority of deaths at work are avoidable and in fact the result of employers ignoring the rules for the provision of safety equipment or training. The HSE has also argued that 70% of these deaths could have been avoided by positive action on the part of employers.

There is thus strong evidence that at least some companies may have been guilty of reckless or negligent killing, which would amount to manslaughter under English law. None have even been charged. One reason for this is that the courts have refused to apply a rule of "aggregation", whereby a company may be regarded as criminally liable because of the fault of a number of directors. As the law stands, companies are generally prosecuted under the health and safety legislation where there is sufficient evidence, and not under the common law of manslaughter.

General Offences of Dishonesty

The crime of theft is defined by the Theft Act 1968 as the dishonest appropriation of property belonging to another with the intention to permanently deprive. This means that there need not be a physical taking of property for the offence to be committed. In a recent Hong Kong case, a director dishonestly sold property belonging to his company at a gross undervalue. He was convicted of theft.

It should further be noted that, since the offence refers to "property belonging to another", the fact that a company has its own legal personality means that its assets can, as a matter of law, be stolen.

Section 18 of the Theft Act 1968 states that where an offence is committed by a company under *sections 15, 16* or *17* of the Act, and it is proved to have been committed with the consent or connivance of any director, he as well as the company shall be liable.

The aim of *section 18* is to put directors under a positive obligation to prevent irregularities. The general rule in criminal law is that passive acquiescence does not give rise to criminal liability. But in relation to directors, the criminal law takes the view that their responsibilities require them to take positive steps to intervene to prevent fraud.

Section 18 refers to "section 15, 16 or 17 of this Act".

Section 15 deals with obtaining property by deception. Thus a director who knows that another director is telling lies in order to obtain property, but does nothing about it, may also be guilty of the offence.

Section 16 concerns obtaining a pecuniary advantage by deception — roughly, obtaining credit by fraud — and the same considerations would seem to apply.

Section 17 covers false accounting. It states, in paraphrase, that it is an offence for a person dishonestly, with a view to gain or intent to cause loss, to destroy, deface, conceal or falsify any account or record or document made or required for any accounting purpose; or to produce or make use of any such account, etc which he knows to be misleading, false or deceptive. The maximum sentence for this offence is seven years' imprisonment.

The wording of *section 17* is wide enough to include computer records. The document need not be an account itself, so long as it is used for accounting purposes. The operation of the section is illustrated by *R v Wines* (1953) where an employee falsely overstated the profits made by his department in order to persuade his employer to continue to employ him. This behaviour is clearly covered by section 17. The section includes the requirement that the accused should have acted "dishonestly". This is a highly technical criminal law concept. In general, it is a question of fact to be decided by the jury.

Fraud

There is no offence of fraud in English law. Persons who face allegations of fraudulent behaviour are normally charged with one of the Theft Act offences above, or with conspiracy to defraud.

Conspiracy to defraud is an ancient common law offence of very wide scope, which can cover any dishonest agreement by two or more persons to commit fraud.

In *R v MacDonnell* (1966), M was the sole person responsible for two companies. He was charged with conspiring with the company to defraud others. On appeal, quashing his conviction, it was held that the essence of conspiracy is the acting in concert of two or more persons. Although a company is a separate entity, where the sole responsible person in the company is the accused himself, there cannot be two or more minds, and there is no conspiracy. The true position is that a company and a director cannot be convicted of conspiracy when the only human being who is said to have broken the law or intended to do so is the one director.

Another example involving company directors is *R v Landy* (1981). The chairman of a bank and others were charged with conspiracy to defraud persons dealing with the bank by falsely pretending that the business was being run in an honest and proper manner. Their defence was that they had been careless but honest. The Court of Appeal ruled that dishonesty was an all-important element of the crime of conspiracy to defraud. An assertion by a defendant that throughout a transaction he acted honestly does not have to be accepted but has to be weighed like any other piece of evidence.

Again, in Attorney-General's Reference No. 1 of 1982, the Court of Appeal gave an opinion in a conspiracy to defraud case concerning the production of whisky bottles with false labels for export to the Lebanon. The Court stated that where the aim of a conspiracy was to be carried out abroad, it was not triable in England even if its performance would cause economic loss and damage to the proprietary interests of a company within the jurisdiction, or if its performance would injure person or company here by causing him or it damage abroad.

In *R v Sinclair and Others* (1968) the defendants were charged with conspiracy to cheat and defraud a company, its shareholders and creditors, by fraudulently using its assets for purposes other than those of the company and by fraudulently concealing such use. The conspiracy charge amounted, in effect, to an agreement by a director of the company and others dishonestly to take a risk with its assets in a manner known not to be in the company's best interest and to be prejudicial to minority shareholders. The accused were convicted, and their convictions were upheld by the Court of Appeal, which ruled that it is fraudulent to prejudice another's rights by knowingly taking a risk which no one has a right to take, and it is no defence to claim that one had an honest belief that benefit, not prejudice, would result.

Summary: Potential Criminal Liability of Directors

- Companies Acts offences
- Insolvency Act 1986
- Trade Descriptions Act 1968 and other consumer protection statutes
- Aiding and abetting
- Factories Act 1961
- Health and Safety at Work Act 1974
- Manslaughter
- General offences of dishonesty:

Theft Act 1968:	Stealing
	Deception
	False accounting
Common law:	Conspiracy to defraud

Appendix

Company Insurance

It is a basic rule of insurance law that the insured must have an "insurable interest" in the subject matter of the insurance. A company clearly has an insurable interest in company assets and potential liabilities.

Contracts of insurance are described as being *uberrimae fidei* (based on the utmost good faith). This means that the insurer is under a legal obligation to disclose all relevant facts known to him. Failure to disclose such material facts may invalidate the policy.

It is advisable for specialist companies, or those engaged in unusual business activities, to deal with specialised insurance companies.

The following types of insurance cover are particularly significant for company directors.

Credit Insurance

The aim of this is to protect businesses against losses caused by the failure of the customers, due to insolvency, to pay for goods and services supplied to them. It is available in respect of both domestic and export sales. Protection may be extended to particular customers or to the whole of a company's annual turnover.

Recent economic conditions, with their resulting high level of business failures and company insolvencies, have meant that this type of insurance has become increasingly popular as a means of safeguarding cash flow. But it can be prohibitively expensive.

Employers' Liability Insurance

The Employers' Liability (Compulsory Insurance) Act 1969,

which came into force on 1 January 1972, imposed a duty upon employers to effect insurance in relation to claims for diseases and injuries brought against them by employees, where such injuries or diseases have been suffered in the course of employment.

An employer must display a certificate of insurance at the workplace. Failure to take out such insurance, or to display the certificate, is an offence punishable with a maximum penalty of £1000 or £500 respectively.

Directors employed under a contract of service will automatically be covered by such policies. Directors without such contracts will not normally be covered and the policy should therefore be endorsed to give specific protection to such directors.

Public Liability Insurance

The aim of this type of insurance is to protect companies against legal liability in respect of members of the public arising from its business activities. It resembles employers' liability insurance except that it relates to a wider class of persons than simply employees of the company.

There is no legal obligation to take out public liability insurance, but it is generally thought to be desirable since almost any business activity may involve "risk" to the public.

Product Liability Insurance

This deals specifically with the strict liability imposed by the Consumer Protection Act 1987 upon producers of defective products. It aims to protect firms against legal liability for damage to third parties, including loss of or damage to property, caused by goods which the insured has sold, supplied, repaired or serviced.

Directors' and Officers' Liability Insurance

Policies of this type reflect the law's increasing concern with the strict enforcement of company law in relation to the responsibilities of directors. In summary, the types of liability which may be insured against are as follows.

Statutory Liabilities

- More than two hundred criminal offences set out in the Companies Acts 1985 and 1989.
- Wrongful trading under section 214 of the Insolvency Act 1986.
- Breach of a disqualification order under the Company Directors Disqualification Act 1986.
- Health and safety offences.
- Crimes under the Theft Acts 1968 and 1978.
- Product liability: see the Consumer Protection Act 1987.
- Offences under the Financial Services Act 1986.

Common Law

- General duty of care. The general test is that directors must exercise that degree of care which corresponds to persons of their skill, qualifications and expertise. Breach of this duty will give rise to liability, for example where company funds are lost through a risky investment.

  More specifically, common law duties include:

- Failing to disclose interests in contracts.
- Conflict of interest.
- Transferring shares to others for their own benefit.
- Misappropriation of company property.
- Unauthorised borrowing.

In relation to this class of insurance it is important to note that the following types of director would be well advised to seek cover:

- part-time directors
- shadow directors
- alternate directors
- nominee directors.

The reason for this is that section 741(1) of the Companies Act 1985 defines "director" as including any person who actually occupies the position of director, however that person is described.

Section 137 of the Companies Act 1989 now provides that a company may purchase and maintain insurance for its officers against liability for negligence, default, breach of duty and breach of trust. The fact of such insurance must be disclosed in the directors' report.

Fidelity Insurance

The purpose of fidelity policies is to protect companies against fraud and dishonesty by employees. "Floating" fidelity policies cover all employees without naming individuals. Such policies normally contain a requirement that the insured should operate a proper system of checking and supervision in relation to the honesty of employees.

Commercial Legal Protection

This type of insurance covers legal and other professional expenses incurred in the course of the business. Typically, it may include cover for the following:

- legal expenses resulting from the pursuit or defence of contractual claims
- legal expenses incurred in defending criminal proceedings (limited to those arising from the conduct of the business)
- accountants' fees for dealing with VAT appeals
- legal costs in connection with Inland Revenue investigations. Companies offering commercial legal protection will normally offer a free 24 hour telephone advisory service. This should be contacted before any claims are made or legal steps taken.

Glossary

This glossary of technical terms is designed for use by non-legal professionals in order to make the body of the text more accessible. It covers, in particular, words and phrases with legal meanings which may differ from their everyday meanings, and which are not fully explained in the text. The glossary is intended to meet the demands of those concerned with company administration and directorships for explanations of lawyers' jargon.

ACCOUNT, ORDER FOR	A court order requiring the investigation and payment of sums due from one person to another as the result of a transaction.
ACTION	The formal exercise of a legal right.
ADMINISTRATION	The formal process of managing the assets and liabilities of an insolvent company.
AGENT	A person who has the power to enter into legally-binding agreements on behalf of another.
AIDING AND ABETTING	Generally, helping a person to commit a criminal offence.
BANKRUPTCY	The insolvency of an individual.
BONA FIDE	In good faith.

BREACH	The infringement of a legal right or duty.
CHARGE	An incumbrance which secures the payment of money.
CIVIL (ACTION, COURT, LAW)	Civil courts are those which deal with private rights, as distinct from those which deal with allegations of crime.
COMMON LAW	The meaning used in this book is that body of law created by judicial decisions rather than by Parliament.
COMPENSATION	Payment for loss or injury sustained.
CONSPIRACY	An agreement by two or more persons to commit an unlawful act.
CONSTRUCTIVE TRUST	A trust (see below) imposed by equity (see below) regardless of the intentions of the parties, in the interests of justice and good conscience.
CONTEMPT OF COURT	Disobedience to the rules of a court; interference with court proceedings.
CONTRACT	The law of contract is the body of rules governing agreements intended to create legal relations.
CONTRIBUTION	Payment of a share of liability.
CONVICTION	A finding of guilt by a criminal court.

COVENANT — A binding promise normally set out in a deed.

CRIME, CRIMINAL — An act, deemed to be an offence against the State, which is punishable.

DAMAGES — Compensation in financial terms for loss or injury suffered by the plaintiff.

DEBENTURE — A document acknowledging indebtedness by a company, usually secured by a charge on the company's property.

DECEIT — A civil wrong (tort) based on a false statement of fact made knowingly or recklessly with the intention that it should be relied upon by a person who suffers damage as a result.

DECLARATION — A remedy whereby a court declares a legal position based upon the facts of a case.

DEED — A written instrument signed, sealed, executed and delivered.

DEEMED — Supposed.

DEFAULT — Failure to carry out a legal requirement.

DEFENDANT — A person who is on the receiving end of legal proceedings.

DELEGATION — The passing of power or authority from one person to another.

DISHONESTY	A question of fact to be decided by the jury in criminal trials.
EQUITY	A body of law developed by the Court of Chancery.
EXECUTOR	A person appointed by a will to carry out its terms.
FIDUCIARY DUTY	The relationship of trust or confidence owed by a director to a company.
FRAUD	Intentional or reckless deceit.
FREEHOLD	An interest in land with an indeterminate duration.
GROSS NEGLIGENCE	Really serious negligence, amounting to total indifference to consequences.
GUARANTEE	A promise to meet another person's debt.
HOLDING COMPANY	A company which has a controlling interest in another company.
IMPLIED TERM	A term of a contract, not expressly set out, which is presumed by the law to reflect the intentions of the parties.
INDEMNITY	A contract of indemnity arises when a person promises to give security against the injury or loss which might be suffered by another.

INDICTABLE, INDICTMENT	An indictment is a written statement accusing a person of a criminal offence which is to be tried in the Crown Court before a judge and a jury.
INDUSTRIAL TRIBUNALS	Bodies which deal with a wide range of complaints in the area of employment law, including unfair dismissal, redundancy and discrimination. The tribunal consists of a legally-qualified chairman and two others.
INJUNCTION	An order of a court requiring a person to do or refrain from doing a particular thing.
INSOLVENCY	Inability to pay debts.
INTENTION	A mental state in which a person foresees and wishes the consequences of his conduct.
INTERLOCUTORY	Not final: during the course of legal proceedings.
LEASE	An interest in land which confers exclusive possession for a fixed period of time.
LIABILITY	Legal obligation or duty.
LIQUIDATOR	A person who is appointed to wind up a company.
LOCUS STANDI	The right to be heard in legal proceedings.

MISFEASANCE	The improper performance of a legal duty.
MISREPRESENTATION	The making of a false statement as to a relevant fact.
NEGLIGENCE	A technical legal concept, generally meaning careless conduct, but subject to strict and complex legal rules.
OFFENCE	A crime. (See above.)
PLAINTIFF	A person who commences legal proceedings.
PRINCIPAL	A person on whose behalf an agent makes a contract.
PROCEDURE	The formal method of conducting legal proceedings.
PROSECUTION	The institution of proceedings in the criminal courts.
QUASH	A decision by a court that a decision is void.
QUORUM	A specified number of persons who must be present in order to validate proceedings of a body of persons.
RECEIVER	A person appointed to ensure the payment of debts.
RELIEF	The remedial action of a court.
REMEDY	Legal means of recovering rights or obtaining redress or compensation.

REPEAL	To revoke or rescind.
REPUDIATION	The refusal to accept the terms of a binding contract.
RESCISSION	The revocation or abrogation of a contract.
SECURITIES	Shares, debentures, debenture stock, loan stock, income notes, income stock, funding certificates and securities of a like nature.
SELF-INCRIMINATION	A person answering questions when the replies might lead to prosecution.
STATUTE	An Act of Parliament, passed by the House of Commons and House of Lords and signed by the Sovereign.
SUBSIDIARY COMPANY	A company which is controlled by another company, either by membership or by holding more than half of its share capital.
SUMMARY	An offence which may only be dealt with in the magistrates' court.
TORT	The branch of law dealing with liability for civil wrongs. The normal remedy for a tort is damages as compensation for the wrong done, or an injunction to prevent repetition of the wrong.

TRUST	An obligation in equity which imposes duties upon a trustee to deal with property for the benefit of a beneficiary.
ULTRA VIRES	Beyond the power. Normally applied to the acts of companies or public bodies.
VOID	Of no legal effect.
VOIDABLE	Capable of being made void but not necessarily so.

Further Information

Could You Use Additional Copies of this Book?

Croner's Guide to Directors' Responsibilities is a pocket book designed for practical use by all those with or intending to take on a director's responsibilities. If you are a subscriber to *Croner's Reference Book for Employers* this is the third of four free books on key areas of employment.

Are there other directors in your organisation or managers who will become directors, who would benefit from having a copy to hand? If so, why not give them a copy to help them to consolidate their knowledge or to understand the responsibilities they are about to take on.

Further Reading

Becoming a Director — What you need to know (Coopers & Lybrand)

The Company Director and the Law, J. A. Franks (Longman)

Company Directors: Liabilities, Rights and Duties, C. L. Ryan (CCH Editions)

Croner's Health and Safety Case Law (Croner Publications, 1992)

Gore-Browne on Companies (Jordans, 1992)

How to know your rights at work, R. Spicer (How To Books, 1991)

Palmer's Company Law (Sweet & Maxwell, 1992)

Reference Book for the Self-Employed and Smaller Business (Croner Publications, 1992)

Rights and Duties of Directors, D. Wright (Butterworths)

Secretarial Administration (Jordans, 1992)

Other Books

You may not be aware of the many books we publish on subjects of interest and relevance to employers. The broad range of topics covered reflect the breadth of your responsibilities and interests.

Our books always take a practical approach and are written with the non-specialist in mind. Jargon-free language, the essential facts and a clear format ensure that these books meet your needs.

Here are some of the titles we publish:

Introduction to Employment Law
by Robert Upex
Price: £19.95
ISBN: 1 85452 063 6

Protecting your Business and Confidential Information
by Audrey Williams
Price £10.95
ISBN: 1 85524 109 9

Procedure in Industrial Tribunal Cases
by Vivian Du-Feu
Price £12.95
ISBN: 1 85525 108 0

Collective Labour Law
by Martin Warren
Price £10.95
ISBN: 1 85524 107 2

Psychometric Testing in Personnel Selection and Appraisal
by Paul Kline
Price £19.95
ISBN: 1 85524 112 9

The Role of the Pension Fund Trustee
by John Cunliffe
Price £15.95

ISBN: 1 85524 0921 2

Debt Recovery in the County Court
by Michael Barry
Price £19.95
ISBN: 1 85524 118 8

Dictionary of Payroll Terms
by Derek French
Price £14.95
ISBN: 1 85524 162 5

For further details contact our Customer Services team on 081–547–3333 quoting reference SV3.

Conferences and Training

Attending a seminar is one of the best ways of keeping up with rapidly changing legislation, trends and new ideas. Croner Conferences and Training have 10 years experience of running an extensive range of courses, from three-day residential to one-day seminars, all led by authoritative and experienced speakers.

Courses are regularly offered on the following subjects:

Handling Disciplinary Situations and Interviews

The Effective Secretary

Going to Tribunal

Concise Guide to Employment Law

Drafting Contracts of Employment

Absenteeism

Statutory Sick Pay

SMP and Other Maternity Rights

The Effective Personnel Assistant

Introduction to Employment Law

Fair Dismissal — The 'Dos and Don'ts'

INDEX